ISBN 978-1-330-62525-5
PIBN 10084112

English
Français
Deutsche
Italiano
Español
Português

www.forgottenbooks.com

Mythology Photography **Fiction**
Fishing Christianity **Art** Cooking
Essays Buddhism Freemasonry
Medicine **Biology** Music **Ancient
Egypt** Evolution Carpentry Physics
Dance Geology **Mathematics** Fitness
Shakespeare **Folklore** Yoga Marketing
Confidence Immortality Biographies
Poetry **Psychology** Witchcraft
Electronics Chemistry History **Law**
Accounting **Philosophy** Anthropology
Alchemy Drama Quantum Mechanics
Atheism Sexual Health **Ancient History**
Entrepreneurship Languages Sport
Paleontology Needlework Islam
Metaphysics Investment Archaeology
Parenting Statistics Criminology
Motivational

AGGRESSIVE CHRISTIANITY.

PRACTICAL SERMONS

BY

MRS. CATHERINE BOOTH,

WITH AN INTRODUCTION BY

DANIEL STEELE, D. D.

BOSTON:
McDONALD & GILL,
OFFICE OF THE CHRISTIAN WITNESS,
36 BROMFIELD ST.

31788

PUBLISHERS' PREFACE.

Our attention was first called to this book by Rev. Daniel Steele, D. D., and after a careful, and, to us, profitable reading, we yielded readily to his persuasion to give it to the American Churches, being assured that its practical, burning truths, must arouse all to a clearer apprehension of their duty and privilege.

These sermons are a marvel of direct, earnest appeal to the hearts of all who seek to know the way of the Lord more perfectly. No one can read them without being profoundly stirred, and scripturally enlightened. They are suited to arouse the dormant energies of all classes to a better and more useful life.

The Introduction, by Dr. Steele, sets forth in earnest words the religious character of the author, and the excellencies of these sermons. We give them to the public with the prayer that their perusal may kindle a flame of revival in all the land by stirring up the people to seek the pentecostal baptism.

McDONALD & GILL

enemies of all classes to n `

AUTHOR'S PREFACE.

The addresses contained in this little volume were delivered during a series of services at the West End of London, in the summer of 1880. That they were used then of the Lord I had abundant evidence, and on that account I have consented to their reproduction in this form, hoping that He may still speak through them to many souls.

I only regret that pressing public duties have prevented the shorthand writer's notes being revised as thoroughly as I could have wished, especially as they are reports of what were themselves largely unpremeditated utterances.

CATHERINE BOOTH.

London, December, 1880.

INTRODUCTION.

This volume is reprinted in America at my oft-repeated suggestion. When the reader has finished these sermons he will not ask why I have urged the publication of an American edition. The sermons will have spoken for themselves. To induce the Christian public to read this book, a few words of information respecting its gifted author, her excellencies as a preacher, and the wonderful work in which she is engaged, will be our only argument.

Mrs. Catherine Booth is the wife of Rev. William Booth, formerly a Primitive Methodist preacher, but now the Commander-in-Chief of the Salvation Army. Converted at fifteen, her piety till several years after her marriage was like a shaded lamp, shining only upon the narrow circle of the parsonage and parish. She says: "I was one of the most timid and bashful disciples the Lord Jesus ever saved." For ten years the daily battle of her life was with the duty of giving public testimony with her lips to the power of Christ to save. Her victory at last, and her re markable call to preach when the mother of four children under five years of age, and the spiritual power of her ministry, are thrillingly detailed in the sermon on "Witnessing for Christ." She has been a preacher twenty-three years, and has brought up nine children to preach the Gospel.

My first knowledge of Mrs. Booth was obtained in 1880, from a letter of a strait-laced Presbyterian doctor of divinity, published in one of the organs of that denomination in New York. He had listened to all the celebrities in London, not excepting Spurgeon and Parker, but had heard no speaker who had moved him so deeply as a woman preaching in a hall in the West End of London. The woman was Mrs. Booth. This confession by a minister who would have been subjected to ecclesiastical censure if he had introduced a woman into his own pulpit, so excited my interest that I began to inquire about this new light which had arisen upon England, and to wonder whether the printing press would not soon reflect its rays upon our western world. I could not wait for an American reprint, but immediately sent for the volumes of her sermons. Having feasted upon them for several months, I am constrained to invite my fellow-Christians in America to the banquet. The volume entitled "Godliness" is not on the table, but is in course of preparation by McDonald & Gill, and will be eagerly sought for by all who have tasted of " Aggressive Christianity."

One of the bishops of the Church of England has recently issued a letter to the clergy of his diocese, urging them, if they would be aroused and stimulated to go out and compel the unchurched and perishing masses to come to the gospel feast, to study the discourses of Mrs. Booth. Here they would find inspiration and incentives to this long-neglected work.

The relation of Mrs. Booth to the Salvation Army may lead some to suppose that her sermons are only frothy rantings addressed to vicious and illiterate crowds, "the unwashed mob" of the metropolis of England. This is a great mistake. While General Booth was preaching in Mile End, letting down the Gospel plummet to sound the depths of the slums in eastern London, his wife was gathering the cultured and aristocratic class in the western part of the city, attracting such intellects as Frances Power Cobbe, · the admirer and correspondent of Theodore Parker. This Unitarian lady, whose fame as a *literateur* has reached all parts of the English-speaking world, says of Mrs. Booth's preaching: " The combination of fervent zeal with practical good sense, in her extempore discourses, must be admired even by those who differ most widely from her views."

It has been truthfully said that woman excels in insight, in her power of intellectual penetration, in the instantaneous, intuitive discernment of truth, like that of St. John, and that the masculine mind is superior in the discursive, or dialectic faculty, in the Pauline ability to forge and weld together the successive links of a chain of reasoning. Mrs. Booth combines both these qualities. She is Pauline and Johannean in the cast of her mind. He will be happily disappointed who opens this volume expecting to find only what Renan sneeringly styles — when he characterizes the resurrection message of Mary Magdalene — "the hallucination of an excited woman's imagination." The reader must look elsewhere for the gospel of gush. In these sermons there is no incoherency, no rhapsody, no rhodomontade, but sound theology in consecutive propositions set forth in natural and logical sequence according to the laws of thought, the whole delivered with Divine unction, a river of truth set on fire by the Holy Ghost, bearing down or burning up everything before it. One element of her power is her plain, stout, terse Saxon speech, not slang, but the language of the home, the shop, and the street. Her sermons are theology in homespun. She eschews a scholastic form of theology in buckram and broadcloth.

This volume is rightly named. For two reasons the subject of the first sermon may well be applied to the entire book. First, the preacher insists that the Gospel, when it enters the heart, should be aggressive till it conquers the last lurking foe, through the power of the Holy Spirit wholly sanctifying it by an instantaneous finishing stroke given to original sin, as taught by John Wesley. This is a cardinal doctrine of the Salvation Army, and the secret of its conquering power. A meeting specially for the promotion of this experience is held weekly in every one of their barracks.

In the second place, the Gospel is to be aggressive till it subdues the whole world to Jesus, its rightful King. The mighty faith of Mrs. Booth grasps this glorious consummation, as within the reach of the present generation of believers, if they yield themselves fully to the impulses of the Holy Spirit. She is no gloomy pessimist, bewailing the decay of Christianity and dishonoring the dispensation of the Paraclete by postponing the world's conversion till after Jesus shall descend from Heaven, and in person set up a visible kingdom on the earth. These sermons are a healthful antidote to this paralyzing error, and a mighty stimulus to missionary activity. Christians are exhorted to a grand evangelistic assault upon whole communities, imposing the Gospel upon them. While I am writing, detachments of the Salvation Army are attacking all the principal towns in

England and Scotland, and columns are marching on France, Sweden, Switzerland, North America, South Africa, and India. They exemplify their own doctrines respecting the two-fold aggressive power of Christianity. They have lifted it out of its century-worn ruts, put a steam-engine behind it, and set it running everywhere at will, like a pioneer's wagon on a wild prairie. God speed the new Gospel chariot, till it bears King Jesus round the world!

Long have we mourned over the religious apathy which deadens the zeal of American Christianity. On all her church doors have I, in thought, seen this advertisement:—

WANTED!

RELIGIOUS ENTHUSIASM.

Inquire within.

This book comes knocking at these church doors with ability to answer this universal call. If Christians would read it and become imbued with the spirit of its consecrated author, there would be an uprising of a slumbering host and a spiritual Waterloo would ensue, "putting to flight the armies of the aliens."

An English essayist has well said: " A great evil, to which human beings are by their make subject, is, that they can talk of things, know things, and understand things, without *feeling* them in their true importance — without, in short, *realizing* them. There appears to be a certain numbness about the mental organs of perception; and the man who is able to *put things* so strikingly, clearly, pithily, forcibly, glaringly, whether these things are religious, social, or political truths, as to get through that numbness, that crust of insensibility, to the quick of the mind and heart, must be a great man, an earnest man, an honest man, a good man. I believe that any great reformer will find less practical discouragement in the opposition of bad people, than in the *inertia* of good people." At just this point lies the obstacle to the advance of the Gospel. All forcible opposition has ceased, but a greater peril threatens us — "the *inertia* of good people." The sermons which I am now introducing to the good people of America have this desirable quality, they pierce religious numbness to the quick, and make the mind REALIZE Gospel truth. May this realization inspire intense activity in plucking lost men as brands from the eternal burnings!

I have often endeavored in imagination to transport myself to the first Christian century, when Christianity in the zeal of her Pentecostal baptism, was going forth as an army unincumbered with a baggage train and a host of non-com·

batants, to conquer the world. I have always failed to re
produce the scene. The sermons of this eloquent woman
now come to my help. They show me what Christianity is
when stripped of a cumbersome ceremonialism, a deadening
formalism, a crushing ecclesiasticism, cut loose from the baggage train of church debts engineered by rich and worldly
men, and relieved of a host of nominal Christians impeding
her march, pleased only with dress parades, and raising a
panic whenever the sham fight for a moment becomes real.
I now see as with anointed vision that a regenerated Christianity would speedily conquer the world. John Goodwin,
more than two centuries ago, saw the need of a doctrinal regeneration of Christianity, clearing it from the errors of
Calvinism. He wrote his "Redemption Redeemed, wherein
the most glorious Work of Redemption of the World by
Jesus Christ is vindicated by the Encroachments of latter
Times." A similar work has Mrs. Booth wrought in her
sermons, in her Redemption of the Gospel from its bondage
to enfeebling proprieties and churchly fashions and unspirit-
ual and worldly tastes and maxims. She has demonstrated
that the simple Gospel, preached in faith in the streets of
London, without the sanction of ecclesiastical or civil authority, without wealth, without learning and the patronage
of the upper classes, is just as powerful as it was when it

stood up alone in the streets of Jerusalem, leaning only on the arm of a Jewish fisherman, stammering with a Galilean brogue.

DANIEL STEELE.

Peabody, March 1, 1883.

CONTENTS.

17

AGGRESSIVE CHRISTIANITY.

Go ye into all the world and preach the Gospel to every creature. — MARK
xvi. 15.
And I said, Who art thou, Lord? And He said, I am Jesus whom thou perse-
cutest. But rise, and stand upon thy feet : for I have appeared unto thee
for this purpose, to make thee a minister and a witness both of these things
which thou hast seen, and of those things in the which I will appear unto
thee : Delivering thee from the people, and from the Gentiles, unto whom
now I send thee, to open their eyes, and to turn them from darkness to
light, and from the power of Satan unto God, that they may receive forgiveness of sins, and inheritance among them which are sanctified by faith
that is in me. — ACTS xxvi. 15-18.

Suppose we could blot out from our minds all knowledge
of the history of Christianity from the time of this Inaugu-
ration Service — from that Pentecostal Baptism — or, at any
rate, from the close of the period described in the Acts of
the Apostles ; suppose we could detach from our minds all
knowledge of the history of Christianity since then, and
take the Acts of the Apostles and sit down and calculate
what was likely to happen in the world, what different results we should have anticipated, what a different world we
should have reckoned upon as the outcome of it all. A
system which commenced under such auspices, with such
assumptions and professions on the part of its Author (speaking after the manner of men), and producing, as it did, in
the first century of its existence, such gigantic and moment-
ous results. We should have said, if we knew nothing of
what has intervened from that time to this, that, no doubt,
the world where that war commenced, and for which it was
organized, would have long since been subjugated to the in-

19

fluence of that system, and brought under the power of its great Originator and Founder! I say, from reading these Acts, and from observing the spirit which animated the early disciples, and from the way in which everything fell before them, we should have anticipated that ten thousand times greater results would have followed, and, in my judgment, this anticipation would have been perfectly rational and just.

We Christians profess to possess in the Gospel of Christ a mighty lever which, rightly and universally applied, would lift the entire burden of sin and misery from the shoulders, that is, from the souls, of our fellow-men—a panacea, we believe it to be, for all the moral and spiritual woes of humanity, and in curing their spiritual plagues we should go far to cure their physical plagues also. We all profess to believe this. Christians have professed to believe this for generations gone by, ever since the time of which we have been reading, and yet, look at the world, look at so-called Christian England and America, in this end of the nineteenth century! The great majority of the nations utterly ignoring God, and not even making any pretence of remembering Him one day in a week. And then, look at the rest of the world. I have frequently got so depressed with this view of things that I have felt as if my heart would break. I don't know how other Christians feel, but I can truly say that "rivers of water do often run down my eyes because men keep not His law," and because it seems to me that this dispensation, compared with what God intended it to be, has been, and still is, as great a failure as that which preceded it.

Now, I ask, how is this? I do not for a moment believe that this is in accordance with the purpose of God. Some people have a very convenient way of hiding behind God's purposes, and saying, "Oh! He will do His own will." I wish He did! They say, "You know God's will is done after all." I wish it were! *He* says it is *not* done, and over and over again laments the fact that it is not done. He wants it to be done, but it is NOT DONE! "It is of no use to stand up and propound theories that are at variance with things as they are." There has been a great deal too much of this, and it has had a very bad effect. The world is in this con-dition, and here is a system launched under such auspices, with such purposes, with such promises, and with such pros-pects, and yet nearly nineteen hundred years have rolled away and here we are. How little has been done, com-paratively. What a little alteration has been effected in the habits and dispositions of the race.

But some of you will say, "Well, but there is a good deal done." Thank God for that. It would be sad if there were *nothing* done; but it looks like a drop in the ocean compared with what should have been done. Now I cannot accept any theory which so far reflects upon the love and goodness of God as to make *Him* to blame for this effeteness of Chris-tianity, and, so far as my influence extends, I will not allow the responsibility and the blame of all this to be rolled back upon God, who so loved the world that He gave His only Son to ignominy and death in order to redeem it. I do not believe it for a moment. I believe that the old arch-enemy has done in this dispensation what he did in former ones — so far circumvented the purposes of God, that he has suc-ceeded in bringing about this state of things — in retarding the accomplishment of God's purposes and keeping the world thus largely under his own power and influence, and I believe he has succeeded in doing this, as he has succeeded always before, by DECEIVING GOD'S OWN PEOPLE. He has always done so. He has always got up a caricature of God's real thing, and the nearer he can get it to be like the original the more successful he is. He has succeeded in deceiving God's people : —

First : — AS TO THE STANDARD OF THEIR OWN RELIGIOUS LIFE.

And, *Secondly,* he has succeeded in deceiving them AS TO THEIR DUTIES AND OBLIGATIONS TO THE WORLD.

He has succeeded, first, in deceiving them as to the standard of their own religious life. He has got the Church, nearly as a whole, to receive what I call an "Oh, wretched man that I am" religion! He has got them to lower the standard which Jesus Christ Himself established in this Book — a standard, not only to be aimed at, but to be attained unto — a standard of victory over sin, the world, the flesh, and the devil, *real, living, reigning, triumphing Christianity!* Satan knew what was the secret of the great success of those early disciples. It was their whole-hearted devotion, their absorbing love to Christ, their utter abnegation of the world. It was their entire absorption in the salvation of their fellowmen and the glory of their God. It was an enthusiastic religion that swallowed them up, and made them willing to become wanderers and vagabonds on the face of the earth — for His sake to dwell in dens and caves, to be torn asunder, and to be persecuted in every form.

It was this degree of devotion, before which Satan saw he had no chance. Such people as these, he knew, must ultimately subdue the world. It is not in human nature to stand before that kind of spirit, that amount of love and zeal, and if Christians had only gone on as they began long since, the glorious prophecy would have been fulfilled. The kingdoms of this world would have become the kingdoms of our lord and of his Christ.

Therefore, the arch-enemy said, "What must I do? I shall be defeated after all. I shall lose my supremacy as the god of this world. What shall I do? No use to bring in a gigantic system of error, which everybody will see to be error." Oh, dear, no! That has never been Satan's way; but his plan has been to get hold of a good man here and there, who shall creep in, as the Apostle said, unawares, and preach another doctrine, and who shall deceive, if it were possible, the very elect. *And he did it.* He accomplished his design. He gradually lowered the standard of Christian life and character, and though, in every revival, God has raised it again to a certain extent, we have never got back thoroughly to the simplicity, purity, and devotion set before us in these Acts of the Apostles and in the Epistles. And just in the degree that it has approximated thereto, in every age, Satan has got somebody to oppose and to show that this was too high a standard for human nature, altogether beyond us, and that, therefore, Christians must sit down and just be content to be "Oh! wretched man that I am" people to the end of their days. He has got the Church into a condition that makes one sometimes positively ashamed to hear professing Christians talk, and ashamed, also, that the world should hear them talk. I do not wonder at thoughtful, intelligent men being driven from such Christianity as this. It would have driven me off, if I had not known the *power* of godliness. I believe this kind of Christianity has made more infidels than all the infidel books ever written.

Yes, Satan knew that he must get Christians down from the high pinnacle of whole-hearted consecration to God. He knew that he had no chance till he tempted them down from that blessed vantage ground, and so he began to spread those false doctrines, to counteract which John wrote his epistles, for. before he died, he saw what was coming, and sounded down the ages : — "Little children, let no man deceive you : he that doeth righteousness is righteous, even as he is righteous. He that committeth sin is of the devil; for the devil sinneth from the beginning. For this purpose the Son of God was manifested, that he might destroy the works of the devil." The Lord revive that doctrine! Help us afresh to put up the standard!

Oh! the great evil is that dishonest-hearted people, because they feel it condemns them, lower the standard to their miserable experience. I said, when I was young, and I repeat it in my maturer years, that if it sent me to hell I would never pull it down. Oh! that God's people felt like that. There is the glorious standard put before us. The power is proffered, the conditions laid down, and we CAN all attain it if we will; but if we will not — for the sake of the children, and for generations yet unborn, do not let us drag it down, and try to make it meet our little, paltry, circumscribed experience. LET US KEEP IT UP. This is the way to get the world to look at it. Show the world a real, living, self-sacrificing, hard-working, toiling, triumphing religion, and the world will be influenced by it; but anything short of that they will turn round and spit upon!

Secondly :— Satan has deceived even those whom he could not succeed in getting to lower the standard of their own lives with respect to their duties and obligations to the world.

I have been reading of late the New Testament with special reference to the aggressive spirit of Primitive Christianity, and it is wonderful what floods of light come upon you when you read the Bible with reference to any particular topic on which you are seeking for help. When God sees you are panting after the light, in order that you may use it, *He pours it in upon you.* It is an indispensable condition of receiving light that you are willing to follow it. People say they don't see this and that, no, because they do not wish to see. They are not willing to walk in it, and, therefore, they do not get it; but those who are willing to obey shall have all the light they want.

It seems to me that we are come infinitely short of any right and rational idea of the aggressive spirit of the New Testament saints. Satan has got Christians to accept what I may call a namby-pamby, kid-glove kind of system of presenting the gospel to people. " Will they be so kind as to read this tract or book, or would they not like to hear this popular and eloquent preacher? They will be pleased with him quite apart from religion." That is the sort of half-frightened, timid way of putting the truth before unconverted people, and of talking to them about the salvation of their souls. It seems to me this is utterly antagonistic and repugnant to the spirit of the early saints : " Go ye and preach the gospel to EVERY CREATURE;" and again the same idea—" Unto whom now I send thee." Look what is implied in these commissions. It seems to me that no people have ever yet fathomed the meaning of these two Divine commissions. I believe the Salvation Army have come nearer to it than any people that have ever preceded them. Look at them. Would it ever occur to you that the language meant, " Go and build chapels and churches and invite the people to come in, and if they will not, let them alone." " GO YE." If you sent your servant to do something for you, and said, " Go and accomplish that piece

of business for me," you know what it would involve.
You know that he must see certain persons, running about
the city to certain offices and banks, and agents, involving a
great deal of trouble and sacrifice; but you have nothing to
do with that. He is *your servant*. He is employed by you
to do that business, and you simply commission him to "Go
and do it." What would you think if he went and took
an office and sent out a number of circulars inviting your
customers or clients to come and wait on his pleasure, and
when they chose to come, just to put your business before
them? No, you would say, "Ridiculous." Divesting our
minds of all conventionalities and traditionalisms, what
would the language mean? "Go ye!" "To whom?"
"To every creature." "Where am I to get at them?"
WHERE THEY ARE. "Every creature." There is the
extent of your commission. Seek them out; run after them,
wherever you can get at them. "Every creature" —
wherever you find a creature that has a soul — there go and
preach my Gospel to him. If I understand it, *that* is the
meaning and the spirit of the commission.

And then again, to Paul, he says, "Unto whom now I
send thee, to open their eyes, *and* to turn *them* from darkness to light, and *from* the power of Satan unto God."
They are asleep — go and wake them up. They do not see
their danger. If they did, there would be no necessity for
you to run after them. They are *preoccupied*. Open their
eyes, and turn them round by your desperate earnestness
and moral suasion and moral force; and, oh! what a great
deal one man can do for another, it makes me tremble to
think! "Turn them from darkness to light, and from the
power of Satan unto God. How did Paul understand it?
He says, "We persuade men." Do not rest content with

just putting it before them, giving them gentle invitations, and then leaving them alone. He ran after them, poor things, and pulled them out of the fire. Take the bandage off their eyes which Satan has bound round them; knock and hammer and burn in, with the fire of the Holy Ghost, your words into their poor, hardened, darkened hearts, until they begin to realise that they are IN DANGER; that there is something amiss. Go after them. If I understand it, that is the spirit of the Apostles and of the early Christians; for we read that when they were scattered by persecution, they "went *everywhere*, preaching the Word." The laity, the new converts, the young babes in Christ. It does not mean always in set discourses, and public assemblies, but they went after men and women, like ancient Israel— "Every man after his man," to try and win him for Christ.

Some people seem to think that the Apostles laid the foundations of all the churches. They are quite mistaken. Churches sprang up where the Apostles had never been. The Apostles went to visit and organise them after they had sprung up, as the result of the work of the early laymen and women going everywhere and preaching the Word. Oh! may the Lord shower upon us in this day the same spirit! We should build churches and chapels; we should invite the people to them; but do you think it is consistent with these two commissions, and with many others, that we should rest in this, when three parts of the population utterly ignore our invitations and take no notice whatever of our buildings and of our services? *They will not come to us.* That is an established fact. What is to be done? They have souls. You profess to believe that as much as I do, and that they must live for ever. Where are they going? What is to be done? Jesus Christ says, "Go after them."

When all the civil methods have failed; when the genteel invitations have failed; when one man says that he has married a wife, and another that he has bought a yoke of oxen, and another that he has bought a piece of land — then does the Master of the feast say, "The ungrateful wretches, let them alone!" "No." He says, "Go out into the highways and hedges, and compel them to come in, that my house may be filled. I will have guests, and if you can't get them in by civil measures, use military measures. Go and COMPEL them to come in." It seems to me that we want more of this determined, aggressive spirit. Those of you who are right with God — you want more of this spirit to thrust the truth upon the attention of your fellowmen.

People say, you must be very careful, very judicious. You must not thrust religion down people's throats. Then, I say, you will never get it down. What! am I to wait till an unconverted, Godless man *wants* to be saved before I try to save him? He will never want to be saved till the death-rattle is in his throat. What! am I to let my unconverted friends and acquaintances drift down quietly to damnation, and never tell them about their souls, until they say, "If you please, I want you to preach to me!" Is this anything like the spirit of early Christianity? No. Verily we must *make* them look — tear the bandages off, open their eyes, make them bear it, and if they run away from you in one place, meet them in another, and let them have no peace until they submit to God and get their souls saved. This is what Christianity *ought* to be doing in this land, and there are plenty of Christians to do it. Why, we might give the world such a time of it that they would get saved in very *self defence*, if we were only up and doing, and determined that they should have no peace in their sins. Where is our zeal for the Lord? We talk of Old Testament saints, but I would we were all like David. "Rivers of water ran down his eyes because men kept not the Law of his God." But you say, "We cannot all hold services." Perhaps not. Go as you like. Go as quietly and softly as the morning dew. Have meetings like the Friends, if you like. ONLY DO IT. Don't let your relatives, and friends, and acquaintances die, and their blood be found on your skirts! ! !

I shall never forget the agony depicted on the face of a young lady who once came to see me. My heart went out to her in pity. She told me her story. She said, "I had a proud, ungodly father, and the Lord converted me three years before his death, and, from the very day of my conversion, I felt I ought to talk to him, and plead, and pray with him about his soul, but I could not muster up courage. I kept intending to do it, and intending to do it, until he was taken ill. It was a sudden and serious illness. He lost his mind, and died unsaved," and she said, "I have never smiled since, and I think I never shall any more." Don't be like that. Do it quietly, if you like; privately, if you like; but do it, and do it as if you felt the value of their souls, and as if you intended to save them, if by any possible means in your power it could be done.

I had been speaking in a town, in the West of England, on the subject of *responsibility* of Christians for the salvation of souls. The gentleman with whom I was staying had winced a bit under the truth, and instead of taking it to heart in love, and making it the means of drawing him nearer to God, and enabling him to serve Him better, he said, "I thought you were rather hard on us this morning." I said, "Did you? I should be very sorry to be harder on anybody than the Lord Jesus Christ would be." He said, "You can push things to extremes, you know. You were talking about seeking souls, and making sacrifices. Now, you are aware that we build the chapels and churches, and pay the ministers, and if the people won't be saved, we can't help it." (I think he had given pretty largely to a chapel in the town.) I said, "It is very heartless and ungrateful of the people, I grant; but, my dear sir, you would not reason thus in any temporal matter. Suppose a plague were to break out in London, and suppose that the Board of Health were to meet and appropriate all the hospitals and public buildings they could get to the treatment of those diseased, and suppose they were to issue proclamations to say that whoever would come to these buildings should be treated free of cost, and every care and kindness bestowed on them, and, moreover, that the treatment would certainly cure them; but, supposing the people were so blind to their own interests, so indifferent and besotted that they refused to come, and, consequently, the plague was increasing and thousands dying, what would you in the provinces say? Would you say, 'Well, the Board of Health have done what they could, and if the people will not go to be healed, they deserve to perish; let them alone!' No, you would say, 'It is certainly very foolish and wicked of the people, but these men are in a superior position. They understand the matter. They know and are responsible for the consequences. What in the world are they going to do? Let the whole land be depopulated?' No! If the people will not come to them, they must go to the people, and force upon them the means of health, and insist that proper measures should be used for the suppression of the plague." It needed no application. He understood it, and I believe, by the spirit of God, he was enabled to see his mistake, to take it home, and set to work to do something for perishing souls.

Men are preoccupied, and it is for us to go and force it upon their attention. Remember, you can do it. There is some *one soul* that you have more influence with than any other person on earth — some soul, or souls. Are you doing all you can for their salvation? Your relatives, friends, and acquaintances *are* to be rescued. Thank God! we are rescuing the poor people all over the land by thousands. There they are, to be looked at, and talked with, and questioned — people rescued from the depths of sin, degradation, and woe — saved from the worst forms of crime and infamy; and, if He can do that, He can save your genteel friends, if only you will go to them desperately and determinedly. Take them lovingly by the button-hole, and say, "My dear friend, I never spoke to you closely, carefully and prayerfully about your soul." Let them see the tears in your eyes; or, if you cannot weep, let them *hear the tears in your voio* , and let them realize that you feel their danger, and are in distress for them. God will give His Holy Spirit, and they *will be saved.*

I was going to note that both texts imply opposition — for, He adds, "Lo, I am with you always, even to the end of the world." As much as if He had said, "You will have need of my presence. Such aggressive, determined warfare as this will raise all earth and hell against you;" and then He says to Paul, "I will be with thee, delivering thee from the people and the Gentiles unto whom I send thee." Why would they need this? Because the Gentiles would soon be up in arms against him, and indeed they were.

Opposition! It is a bad sign for the Christianity of this

day that it provokes so little opposition. If there was no
other evidence of it being wrong, I should know it from
that. When the Church and the world can jog along comfortably together, you may be sure there is something wrong.
The world has not altered. Its spirit is exactly the same
as it ever was, and if Christians were equally faithful and
devoted to the Lord, and separated from the world, living
so that their lives were a reproof to all ungodliness, the
world would hate them as much as ever it did. It is the
Church that has altered, *not* the world. You say, "We
should be getting into endless turmoil." Yes! "I came
not to bring peace on the earth, but a sword." There
would be uproar. Yes; and the Acts of the Apostles
are full of stories of uproars. One uproar was so great
that the Chief Captain had to get Paul over the shoulders
of the people, lest he should have been torn in pieces.
"What a commotion!" you say. Yes; and, bless God, if
we had the like now we should have thousands of sinners
saved.

"But," you say, "see what a very undignified position
this would bring the Gospel into." That depends on what
sort of dignity you mean. You say, "We should always
be getting into collision with the powers that be, and with
the world, and what very unpleasant consequences would
result." Yes, dear friends, there always have been unpleasant consequences to the flesh, when people were following
God and doing His will. "But," you say, "would'nt it be
inconsistent with the dignity of the Gospel?" It depends
from what standpoint you look at it. It depends upon what
really constitutes the dignity of the Gospel. What does
constitute the dignity of the Gospel? Is it human dignity,
or is it Divine? Is it earthly, or is it heavenly dignity?

It was a very undignified thing, looked at humanly, to die
on the cross between two thieves. That was the most undignified thing ever done in this world, and yet, looked at
on moral and spiritual grounds, it was the grandest spectacle
that ever earth or heaven gazed upon, and methinks that
the inhabitants of heaven stood still and looked over the
battlements at that glorious, illustrious Sufferer, as He hung
there between heaven and earth. The Pharisees, I know,
spat upon the humbled Sufferer, and wagged their heads and
said, "He saved others, himself He cannot save." Ah! but
He was intent on saving others. That was the dignity of
Almighty strength allying itself with human weakness, in
order to raise it. It was the dignity of eternal wisdom
shrouding itself in human ignorance, in order to enlighten
it. It was the dignity of everlasting, unquenchable love,
baring its bosom to suffer in the stead of its rebellious
creature — man. Ah! It was incarnate God standing in
the place of condemned, apostate man — the dignity of love!
love! LOVE!

Oh, precious Saviour! save us from maligning Thy Gospel
and Thy name by clothing it with our paltry notions of
earthly dignity, and forgetting the dignity which crowned
Thy sacred brow as Thou didst hang upon the cross! That
is the dignity for us, and it will never suffer by any gentleman here carrying the Gospel into the back slums or alleys
of any town or city in which he lives. That dignity will
never suffer by any employer talking lovingly to his servant
maid or errand boy, and looking into his eyes with tears of
sympathy and love, and trying to bring his soul to Jesus.
That dignity will never suffer even though you should have
to be dragged through the streets with a howling mob at
your heels, like Jesus Christ, if you have gone into those

streets for the souls of your fellow-men and the glory of God. Though you should be tied to a stake, as were the martyrs of old, and surrounded by laughing and taunting fiends and their howling followers — that will be a dignity which shall be crowned in heaven, crowned with everlasting glory. If I understand it, *that* is the dignity of the Gospel — the dignity of love. I do not envy, I do not covet any other. I desire no other,— God is my witness,— than the dignity of love.

Oh, friends! will you get this baptism of love! Then you will, like the Apostles, be willing to push your limbs into a basket, and so be let down by the wall, if need be, or suffer shipwreck, hunger, peril, nakedness, fire, or sword, or even go to the block itself, if thereby you may extend His kingdom and win souls for whom He shed His blood. The Lord fill us with this love and baptise us with this fire, and then the Gospel will arise and become glorious in the earth, and men will believe in us, and in it. They will feel its power, and they will go down under it by thousands, and, by the grace of God, they SHALL.

A PURE GOSPEL.

And I said, Who art thou, Lord? And He said, I am Jesus whom thou perse-
cutest. But rise, and stand upon thy feet: for I have appeared unto thee
for this purpose, to make thee a minister and a witness both of these things
which thou hast seen, and of those things in the which I will appear unto
thee: Delivering thee from the people, and from the Gentiles, unto whom
now I send thee, to open their eyes, and to turn them from darkness to
light, and from the power of Satan unto God, that they may receive forgiveness of sins, and inheritance among them which are sanctified by faith
that is in me. Whereupon, O king Agrippa, I was not disobedient unto the
heavenly vision: but shewed first unto them of Damascus, and at Jerusalem. and throughout all the coasts of Judea, and then to the Gentiles, that
they should repent and turn to God, and do works meet for repentance.—
ACTS xxvi.15-20.

The *second* indispensable condition we are going to note,
this afternoon, to Aggressive Christianity is, a *Pure
Gospel.* I mean by that, God's own pure metal—the una-
dulterated Gospel of Jesus Christ.

There seems, now-a-days, in the Church and the world, as
many different views of the Gospel as there are of secondary
matters and of minor doctrines. One person has one notion
of the Gospel, another has another, until there has come to
be a fearful distraction in the minds of many who are constantly listening to what is called the Gospel. May God the
Holy Ghost help us to look at it impartially and carefully!

First, let me try to define *what is the Gospel.* "Oh!"
people say, "it is good news." Yes, thank God, it
is good news, indeed—news without which we must all
have been lost. It is the news of the free, measureless, un-

35

deserved, reconciling mercy of God, offered to me through the vicarious, infinite, glorious sacrifice of His Son, to the end that I may BE SAVED from sin here and from Hell hereafter!! But this news involves a great deal. It is the news of a definite, practical end, involving conditions; for, even good news to me, involves certain conditions on my part, if I am to procure the good which the news brings. *Secondly*, I will try to explain the conditions on which the Gospel is available to me.

Let me illustrate this; and I am particularly anxious that you should all understand me. Supposing that a province of this empire were in rebellion against our Sovereign. Supposing that the people of that province had trampled under foot our laws, and set up their own in opposition — and suppose the Queen, in her gracious clemency, desired not to destroy these rebels, but to save them, what would be the necessary and indispensable condition in the very nature of the case, in order for her to save them? Not merely a proclamation of pardon. That would be a glorious movement towards the result, but there would want something else; for a proclamation of pardon merely, whilst the rebels remain in an unchanged state, would only be giving them greater facilities for further rebellion. Evidently, in the nature of the case, it is a necessity that a change of mind should be produced in the rebels themselves, for the Queen not only wants to save them from destruction, but to restore them to allegiance and obedience to herself, and, unless she does this, they will never become dutiful and obedient subjects. There will never be anything but anarchy, confusion and rebellion in that province unless those rebels undergo a change of mind. They must be brought back to allegiance and obedience to the Queen.

Just so with God's proclamation of salvation. The mischief is in us. Take the illustration of the Prodigal Son. The mischief was all in him — not in his father. The father loved him before he went away, and the father loved him afterwards. The father's benevolent heart yearned over him all the time he was away, and many a time, perchance, he went to the roof of his house to look over the expanse of country over which the rebellious lad had gone, and wondered whether he would ever come back. The father's heart was yearning over him all the time. How was it that he could not be reinstated in the father's love and in the family privileges? Because there needed a change of heart — a change of mind in HIM. If he had come back to the old homestead with the same rebellious spirit in him, the same desire to be free from the father's oversight, the same unwillingness to be put under the FATHER'S DOMINION and DISCIPLINE, he would still have been a rebel and a prodigal. In the very nature of the case, until there was the necessary change, a wise and righteous father could not pardon him; he must insist, though he loves him dearly, upon a certain change of mind before he can consistently pardon him.

Just so. The laws of mind are the same when operated upon by either God or man. This is not laying any necessity upon God any more than He has laid upon Himself. He has made us with a certain mental constitution, and therefore He must adapt the conditions and means of our salvation to that mental constitution, otherwise He would reflect upon his own wisdom in having given it to us at the first. Therefore when he purposes to save man He must save him *as man* — not as a beast or a machine! He must save him as man, and he must propound such a scheme as will fit and adapt itself to man's nature. Just as the father might not pardon the prodigal, irrespective of the prodigal's state of mind and heart, so neither can God pardon the sinner irrespective of the state of his mind and heart.

I know, by personal contact with hundreds of souls, that there is an alarming amount of misunderstanding and of what I consider false apprehension of the Gospel of Christ at this point. Hence, you have speakers saying, without anything to guard or qualify their words, "Only believe, and you shall be saved;" "Whosoever believeth hath everlasting life." Blessed and glorious truth, *when rightly applied, and applied to the right characters*, but dangerous error, in my opinion, *when applied indiscriminately to unawakened, unrepenting, rebellious sinners.* I have met with disastrous consequences of this all over the land — so disastrous that I would not like to repeat them here. Now, I say, we should be careful to let the people understand what we mean by the Gospel: I dare not do any other. I am so satisfied of the thousands of souls that are deceived at this point, that, while God gives me voice to speak, I dare not but try to warn them, and show them their fatal mistake.

Returning to our illustration — you say, "The man is, so to speak, dead in trespasses and sins. How can he see his own error? How can he lay down the weapons of rebellion? How can he, by himself, come back to the Father?" Granted. Hence, God, in his wisdom and love, has provided for that incapacity which man has induced by his rebellion, by the gift of His Spirit. You say, "The parallel is not perfect between your illustration and the thing illustrated." No, it is not in that point; because temporal rebels can find out by themselves the insanity and wickedness of their course. They can see where it will lead them. They can see the destructive consequences, and be sorry for the course they have taken. They can lay down their weapons of rebellion, and they can conform to the conditions on which the Queen issues her proclamation. You say, " Yes, they can do it, but man cannot." Of course, because he has so hardened his heart that even if he *can*, he never *will* without the Holy Spirit of God. Hence, God has taken compassion on us, and sent His Spirit into the world for this purpose — "To convince the world of sin, of righteousness, and of judgment." Thus he opens our eyes, and shows us our lost estate. Having, by the Holy Ghost, made us realize our desperate condition, then comes the Gospel to meet us just where we are, on condition that we abandon our evil ways, and do the works meet for repentance, which we are *able to do* by the power of the Holy Spirit, as well as to lay down the weapons of our rebellion and accept of Christ, put our neck under his yoke, and pledge ourselves in heart to FOLLOW HIM ALL THE DAYS OF OUR LIFE. These are the conditions involved, and this is the end the Gospel contemplates, and there you see the Gospel accomplishes its END in this case. The heart of the rebel is won back to its Lord, and the indispensable change has taken place in the *being himself*. He has come back to God. His eyes are opened to see the evil of sin, and the desperate state he is in. Tired of himself, and tired of his evil ways, as the Prodigal was of the swine-yard, he arises, leaves them and goes to his father.

But now I must stop to meet a difficulty which I know will arise in many sincere minds. I feel myself such a tender jealousy for the glory of God, that I do highly respect this feeling in others, and if any one disagrees with my views, or my way of putting them, through a feeling of jealousy for the glory of God, they have my profound respect. You will say, "If we are able to abandon our evil courses, and lay down the weapons of rebellion, is not that saving ourselves?" No, dear friends; it is altogether different. You see it is the indispensable condition of salvation in everyone of the nine passages we read, and in many others — that we abandon our evil ways. Now, what does that mean? A gentleman in a letter to me said, "We cannot save ourselves from heart sins." Granted; but we can *will* to be saved from them. Then, there is a great distinction between those sins of the heart which are involuntary, and those deliberate transgressions of God's law which unregenerate men commit. God requires me to abandon all that I CAN, as a condition of salvation, and then, when He saves He will give me power to abandon all that I could not before. The Prodigal had to come away from the swine-yard, the filth, and the husks, before he got into the father's house, and sat down at the father's feast, but when he had done so, then the father said, "Come in," and he brought the best robe and put it on him, and killed the fatted calf, and put the ring of forgiveness upon his hand. Hence, as the old divines used to put it, "You must wait for the Lord in the path of His ordinances," the path of obedience, as far as is possible to you. And is there any other way? Can the drunkard wait for Him while he abides at his cup? Can the thief wait for Him while he continues in his diabolical trade? Can any man indulging in absolute open sin find the Lord? Must he not, as the Saviour says, cut off that right hand, and pluck out that right eye? He never can cleanse his guilt, but he CAN cut off his hand, and when he does that, the Holy Spirit will come in and apply the Blood, and do the cleansing.

Therefore, you perceive, I take the Gospel to be aiming not merely at saving, but *restoring* us. If it were merely to save me without restoring me, what would it do for me? As a moral agent, if the Gospel fails to PUT ME RIGHT, it will fail eternally to make me happy; and if you were to transplant me before the throne, and put me down in the inner circle of archangels with a sense of wrong in my heart, being morally out of harmony with the laws of God, and the moral laws of the universe, I should be as miserable as if I were in Hell, and should want to get away. I must be MADE RIGHT as well as treated as if I were right. I must be changed as well as justified. This is the Gospel put as clearly in our text as it could be, and also the Epistles written by the Apostle Paul, the great expounder of the doctrine of justification by faith. It was through the lips of the glorified Lord Himself, after He had risen, to the great Apostle of the Gentiles, after the Gospel dispensation was fully opened, that this unmistakable commission was given, " Unto whom I now send thee to open their eyes." What to, their sins? As Peter opened the eyes of the murderers of our Lord, on the Day of Pentecost, " Whom ye have crucified and slain;" driving in the convicting truth of God until, in their agony, they cried out, " WHAT MUST WE DO?" He tore off the bandages which Satan had wrapped around them, and drove them as with the schoolmaster's lash, until he drove them to the cross of the crucified One. " Open their eyes" — that is the first thing. Oh! how my soul has often shrunk and wept under the sense of the awful responsibility this brings upon us Christians. The world is asleep. Yes, friends, your relations, your neighbors — they are asleep. They are preoccupied. They are full of the world, and the things of the world. They will not think — they will not see — they will not look into the Word of Life. Your responsibility comes here tenfold. Go AND WAKE

THEM! YOU CAN DO IT, if you have the Holy Ghost in you!

Some people would have said to the Lord Jesus, "What a great deal you are making of human agency, for, after all, Paul is but a man, and you are setting him to open the eyes of the unconverted, and turn them from darkness to light, and from the power of Satan unto God: are you not making too much of human effort?" But the Lord Jesus knew what He was about. He knew that Paul had a power in him which every really renewed child of God has — the Holy Ghost — to equip him for this work, and He says, " Unto whom now I send thee to *open their eyes.*" Go and awake them to a sense of their danger. Take them, metaphorically speaking, by the collar and shake them and make them realize their peril, as you would if they were asleep in a burning house!! And then when you have awakened them, what are you to do? Leave them alone? No, no, for Christ's sake, no. Take hold of them by the mighty power of your moral suasion and zeal, and love, and energy, and turn them right "round from sin and Satan unto God.".

Jesus Christ set Paul to do this, and *Paul did it.* He says, "Knowing, therefore, the terror of the Lord, we persuade men." His was no meek and mild putting of the truth, and leaving people to do as they liked. "Knowing, therefore, the TERROR of the Lord, we PERSUADE men, because we thus judge that if one died for all, then were all dead;" and, oh! what success the Lord gave him in his desperate enterprise. What multitudes did he persuade, and succeed in turning round from darkness to light, and from the power of Satan unto God! Turn them round! "Oh! but," you say, "if they are turned round from darkness, which represents evil, to light, which represents righteousness, are they not saved?" No, not yet. This is only the change effected in their will, which is beautifully exemplified by Paul in Romans vii.—willing to keep the law, willing to obey God, willing to do His will, and follow Him, yea, struggling, but yet unable, though they are brought round from the voluntary choice or embrace of evil, and the voluntary service of the Devil, round to the voluntary choice and embrace of righteousness and the service of God, they are not yet *able* to do it.

Now, don't say I said they *were* able. Don't misrepresent me, as some people do. I will try to be clear, and I say *there is all the difference in the world between* BEING WILLING TO LET JESUS CHRIST SAVE ME FROM MY SINS, AND SAVING MYSELF FROM THEM. It is exactly this change in the attitude of the will which God demands as a CONDITION OF THE EXERCISE OF HIS POWER. It is so in all the miracles. "Wilt thou be made whole?" He says to the man with the withered hand, "Stretch out thy withered hand." The man might have said, "Lord, what an unreasonable request. Are you come to mock me in my misery?" Oh! but Jesus Christ knew what He wanted in the man. He wanted the response of the MAN'S WILL. He wanted the man to say, "Yes, Lord;" and when he said that, the Lord put the strength into the shoulder-bone, and he stretched it out, and it was made whole. There are many souls just there—they will not say, "Yes, Lord," to some condition which the Spirit puts upon them. I could give you some heart-rending illustrations on this point. I am satisfied that this Gospel-enlightened England of ours is full of people just at this point who come crying, and praying, and longing, as they call it, after God. They come up to Jesus Christ again and again. They try to believe; they want to follow Him, but they are kept back by the right hand and the right eye which the Holy Ghost has told them they must cut off and pluck out before He will receive them. They will not do it, and so they are ever learning, and never able to come to a knowledge of the truth. You must renounce evil in your will. You must *will* to "obey the truth." You must say, "Yes, Lord."

I remember, on one occasion, in the West of England, I had been delivering week-day morning addresses. We had a blessed meeting on this particular day. We began at half-past ten, and the Lord was so with us that He supplied the want of refreshment till we had it at 5.30. He made up for the want of dinner or tea. A gentleman was there, with whose appearance I was struck. He was tall, and intelligent, a man of about forty or forty-five. He knelt down without any emotion, more than deep solemnity, at the end of the Communion rail. I had been talking about the reason people walked in darkness — controversy with the Holy Spirit. I said to him, "My dear sir, have you had a controversy with the Holy Spirit?" "Yes," he said; "I have had one for fifteen years. I am ashamed to say it, and it has eaten up all the joy and power of my Christian life, and I have been a useless cumberer of the ground." I did not know till afterwards that he was a deacon of the church, and had come up there in the sight of all the congregation. I said, "Well, my dear sir, you know the Gospel as well as I do. It is of no use to preach faith to you until you are willing to renounce your idol." He said most emphatically, "I know it." I said, "Are you willing?" Oh, with what tenacity the human heart holds on to its idols! Though he had come up to the rail in the face of that congregation, so deeply was he under the power of the Spirit, yet he hesitated. I said, "Well, my dear sir, you must make up your mind. In your case, it is between the choice of this, whatever it may be, and Christ;" and I retired under the pulpit pillars for a minute, and left him to himself and the Lord. I lifted up my heart to God for him, and then I went back, and said, "Will you renounce it?" and, lifting up his eyes to heaven, and bringing his hand down upon the Communion rail, he said, "By the grace of God, I do," and his whole frame heaved with agony, but he stepped into immediate liberty. His blessed Saviour was waiting with arms wide open. There was only this accursed thing which had stood between them, and when he trampled it under his feet, and was willing to forsake it, as a natural consequence, he sprang into the everlasting arms, and received the assurance of salvation. It was all over the town for the next fortnight. People remarked, "Did you ever see such a change come over a man as has come over Mr. So-and-so; he is like a new man. He prays in the prayer-meeting with such fervor. He was at the chapel doors, speaking to the unconverted, and inviting them to come back. He is visiting up and down the town — why, he's a new man!" Was there any change in the gospel? Had he received any fresh light? It was only the old story — only that he had put away the idol, and trampled under foot that which was keeping the life-power of God out of his soul.

Here is another case. At some services in the West of England, a gentleman largely interested in an unlawful business, came every night for five weeks, and used to sit there, the picture of despair and wretchedness, till after ten o'clock. He went on in this way until his friends thought he would lose his reason. He was walking about his bedroom with his Bible open, kneeling down every now and then, struggling and wrestling and trying to believe; but every time he thought of this ungodly business which he could not give up, despair seized him (for he thought of his money — he thought of the consequences to his family), until at last he said, " Money or no money, I will settle it." He gave it up, came out, and got saved at once.

Now I think these illustrations make clear what I mean, by the abandonment, the turning from the embrace of evil to the embrace of righteousness as an indispensable condition of forgiveness. Hence the Holy Ghost has carefully maintained this order—" to open their eyes and to turn them round from darkness to light, and from the power of Satan unto God, that they may receive forgiveness of sins and an inheritance among them that are sanctified by faith that is in me." You see what a different thing this is to presenting Christ to people just as they are, where they are, *doing what they like.* You see what a different Gospel it comes to, insisting upon a thorough renouncement and abandonment of evil as a condition of Jesus Christ receiving the sinner. This was Paul's Gospel. Will you give me any other definition of it ? Can you explain it in any other way ? Paul goes on to show us how *he* understood : — " Whereupon, O King Agrippa! I was not disobedient unto the heavenly vision, but showed first unto them of Damascus and Jerusalem and then to the Gentiles, they should repent and turn to God, and do works meet for repentance." Was this like saying " *Only believe,*" without respect to any antecedent change of mind ? Can anybody show me anything here in the slightest degree approximating to the Antinomian Gospel which has been grafted on to some other of Paul's utterances ? And yet surely the Apostle could not contradict himself. His writings about faith must be in harmony with this most unmistakable putting of the Gospel to both

Jews and Gentiles. Moreover, did he tell Agrippa and Festus to believe? No, he left them trembling at it, because they were not willing to abandon their sins and put away the accursed thing, but to the Philippian gaoler, who said, "Men and brethren, what must I do?" and who brought them out and began to wash their stripes, thus doing works meet for repentance at once, he said, "Believe on the Lord Jesus Christ and thou shalt be saved." Ah! my friend, you may try to get hold of Christ to your dying hour and at the last be lost, while you are holding on to your idols. If he could have saved us after that fashion we needed no Christ, we could have gone into heaven without a Saviour; but He came to save His people *from their sins*, and while you are in love with your sins you may struggle and tremble as Agrippa and Felix did, and as the young ruler did, and you will meet a similar fate. You must let go your idols and be willing that Jesus should come and save you, not down among the dirt and mud of sin, but lift you out of it, wash you, make you clean, and keep you clean, *circumcise your hearts*, and put His law in them, and then you shall know the gladness of His salvation!

I have some people writing to me in this condition. If they are here let me say to them — This is what you have to do — let go your idols and say as the gentleman said of whom I told you, "Poverty or no poverty, business or no business, position or no position, suffering or prosperity never mind — Christ, Christ, I let go all for Thee!"

Have you forsaken evil? Have you cut off the right hand? Have you plucked out the right eye? I have people coming to me in services of this character, groaning and sometimes worn to skeletons. They tell me they are in distress, they have got into bondage, they want the joy of the Lord and His daily fellowship, and when I ask the reason, they generally say, "Well, I don't know, but it seems to be want of faith." Now I say to such people:—

Now let us see what this want of faith arises from. There must be a cause. I am afraid that sin lieth at the door, and when we come to close quarters we generally find there is some idol, some course of conduct, or some *doubtful* conduct which keeps God out of the soul, and when this is confessed and renounced, people get the presence of God and go away rejoicing in Him. It is so in nearly every case. God does not arbitrarily withdraw Himself from His people. He wants to dwell with them. We are His proper abode. He has promised to come and abide with His people, and if He does not, depend upon it there is something in the Temple offensive to Him, something with which He will not dwell. Will you put that away, and consecrate your hearts this day unto the Lord to be His temple, His temple only, and leave consequences with Him. He will be able to look after His own.

Then, lastly, when you have come to this decision, then look and live; take the final leap into the arms of a crucified Saviour. With some souls who have been the subjects of the drawings of the Spirit for years, the difficulty is in the surrendering their wills. They have learned to reason with God; they have lost the little children's way; they are afraid to take the final leap, and there they stand before the Cross, not conscious of anything between them and Christ. What are *you* to do? What Paul told the Philippian gaoler to do—"Believe on the Lord Jesus Christ;" and you say, "What is that, and how am I to believe?" Wonderful how it has got mystified! Believe what? That

He just means what He says; and that when you come,
He does receive — not He will to-morrow, not He did yesterday, but that He does now, this moment. When did He
receive the sinners who came to Him on earth? When
they came. Just the same will He receive you. "Oh!
but," you say, "I do not feel right." No, of course not.
Do you not see, you are to be saved *by* faith. If you are
to be saved by faith, you must exercise faith before you
will be saved. If it is by faith you are to be saved, you
must believe first, and be saved afterwards, if it is only the
next second. "But," you say, "I do not feel it." No, but
you will feel it when *you have got it.* You must believe it
before you get it, on the testimony of His Word — "I will
in no wise cast you out;" "Him that cometh;" "Now I
come, Lord, I come. I have put away my idols; I have put
away everything that consciously stood between me and
Thee. I *will* to serve Thee, I will to follow Thee, I will to
put my *neck under Thy yoke forever*, asking no more questions,
but being willing for Thee to lead me whithersover Thou wilt.
Now, Lord, I come — Thou dost receive." Leap off the poor
old stranded wreck of your own effort, or your own righteousness, or your own sinfulness, or your own unworthiness, or
anything else of your own, into the glorious lifeboat. It is on
the top of the wave this afternoon — another step, and you
will be in — one bound, and you will feel the loving arms of
your Saviour around you. Faith is trust, TRUST. He will do
for you what he promised. Believe that God does *now accept
you wholly for the sake of the sacrifice of His blessed Son ;* that
He justifies you freely from all things from which you could
not be justified by the law. You stand a condemned, guilty,
hell-bound criminal, and nothing but His free, sovereign mercy can save you. Throw yourself upon this, and the moment

you do so in real faith you will be saved. Perhaps you will
say, as a curate of the Church of England, writing to
me last week, said, "I refuse to be saved by logic." So
did I, and I struggled for six weeks because I refused to
be saved by logic—because I *would* have a living, personal
Christ. I admire your decision, my brother, if you are here,
but let this logic help you; nevertheless, Jesus Christ has
promised, if I come, that He will receive me—then, I do
come, and He does receive me, for He cannot lie. Let that
help you. Faith is not logic, but logic may help faith.

Oh! how I should rejoice if some of you were to launch
into the arms of Jesus this moment. It often happens that
while I am speaking souls *do* get into the ark of God's mercy,
and come, or write to tell me afterwards that the Spirit has
come, and he is crying "Abba Father," and now they KNOW
they have passed from death unto life. They don't want
logic then. It is a matter of demonstration with them.
When you have come up to the place where saving faith is
possible to you, you have no more to do, no more to suffer,
no more to pay. By simple trust we are saved. This is the
way every saint on earth was saved. This is the way every
saint in glory was saved. This is the way we are kept
saved, too, by LIVING, DAILY, OBEDIENT FAITH. The Lord
help you just now. Let the idol go. Put away the ungodly companion. Give up the unlawful business, or the
worldly conformity. Put away whatever has stood between
you and Jesus. Trample it under foot and press through
the crowd of difficulties as the woman did, and go right up
and touch Him with this touch of faith, and you shall LIVE
and KNOW THAT YOU ARE HEALED. Then this Gospel will
be good news indeed to you, and Jesus will be the Author
of salvation to you, because you OBEY HIM!

SERMON III.

ADAPTATION OF MEASURES.

I have chosen five or six different passages, all exhibiting the principle of Adaptation, on which I am to speak. The first is 1 Cor. ix. 20–22 : —

> "And unto the Jew I became as a Jew, that I might gain the Jews; to them that are under the law, as under the law, that I might gain them that are under the law; to them that are without law, as without law (being not without law to God, but under the law to Christ), that I might gain them that are without law."

To them that are without law as without law, but here he carefully guards himself by a parenthesis, lest he should seem to favor a lawless Antinomian gospel, "not without law to God, not independent of the great moral law, but under the law to Christ," in which is fulfilled ALL LAW.

> "To the weak became I as weak, that I might gain the weak : I am made all things to all men, that I might by all means save some."

"To the weak became I as weak," — masterpiece of human humility! Most people want to appear strong, but here is a man coming down, and appearing a weak man, that he might win the weak. *That* is the humility of Jesus Christ. The Lord give us the like spirit! Again, 1 Cor. xii. 4–6 : —

> "Now there are diversities of gifts, but the same spirit; and there are differences of administration, but the same Lord; and there are diversities of operations, but it is the same God which worketh all in all."

Some people want the Spirit to work in everyone alike, and in all times the same, but He *chooses* to have diversities. Again, Galatians iii. 27–28 : —

"For as many of you as have been baptized into Christ have put on Christ. There is neither Jew nor Greek, there is neither bond nor free, there is neither male nor female : for ye are all one in Christ Jesus."

That is, so far as the privileges, duties, and obligations of Christ's kingdom are concerned.   There is neither nationality nor sex; and Galatians v. 6 : —

"For in Christ Jesus neither circumcision availeth anything, nor uncircumcision ; but faith which worketh by love."

All mere ordinances and ceremonies come under circumcision.   And 2 Timothy iv. 2 : —

"Preach the word : be instant in season, out of season ; reprove, rebuke, exhort with all longsuffering and doctrine."

What a hue-and-cry there is because the Salvation Army people save men out of season !   And Jude 22, 23 : —

"And of some have compassion, making a difference : and others save with fear, pulling them out of the fire."

"Oh, no," say some of our conventional friends, "you shall not make a difference !"   Now, in all these six texts, the principle of *Adaptation* is most distinctly laid down.

Now we have spent the two last Sabbath afternoons in trying to point out our view of the characteristics of a pure Gospel, and I think we have succeeded in doing this so clearly that no person who followed us carefully can imagine for a moment that we would hold, or teach, any adaptation of the Gospel itself.   As we stated before, we deemed this so above all adaptation — so above any change, that we would not be responsible for transposing its order, much less altering its matter ; that we would not take a dot off one of the "i's," so sacredly intact do we believe the Gospel of Christ in its matter ought to be kept.   We believe also that the ORDER of God ought to be strictly maintained; that it is as rational and true in philosophy as it is in divinity ; and that the way the Spirit operates upon the minds of men is just the same as ever. This we clearly and most carefully pointed out, so that what we have to say now you will please bear in mind, has nothing to do with the GOSPEL MESSAGE ITSELF. We have tried to show our idea (or what we believe to be the Holy Spirit's idea) of a pure Gospel; but when we come to speak of modes and measures, that is quite another thing. I think, from the texts we have read, and from many others equally plain and relevant, that we find it a most easily gathered truth, running all the way through the New Testament, that forms and ceremonies are nothing except as they embody and express real spiritual life and truth. That circumcision is nothing, and that uncircumcision is nothing; baptism is nothing, and being unbaptized is nothing; the Lord's Supper is nothing, and abstaining from the Lord's Supper is nothing, in itself as a form, for he embraces under circumcision all mere outward forms and ceremonies; and all these are nothing, but "KEEPING THE COMMANDMENTS OF GOD:" that is, you may have all these performed upon you, and regularly perform them yourselves, and be but sounding brass and tinkling cymbals, if you keep not the commandments of God;" for circumcision availeth nothing, in another place, and uncircumcision availeth nothing, but faith — what sort? — that WORKETH BY LOVE: that proves its obedience by its deeds. Therefore, we start with that lying clearly before us as a fundamental truth in every page of the New Testament, that forms and ceremonies, whatsoever they may be, are nothing except as they embody and represent REAL SPIRITUAL LIFE, and truth and action — *action!* Now, it was the great sin — the crowning condemnation of the Jews — that they had frittered away the spirituality and practical bearing of the Divine Law, clinging on to those forms and ceremonies

which were instituted only to embody and symbolise it.
Would to God they had let go the form when they let go
the spirit. Jesus Christ wishes they had. He tells them
it would have been far better. He told them they were
children of the devil, notwithstanding their holding on to
their relationship to Abraham and all the spiritual forms
and ceremonies of their ritual.

They had better have come out and avowed themselves unbelievers, than have gone on professing to be the children
of God while they were doing the work of the devil. But
they would not receive this teaching. It was too cutting for
them, and so they would not have it. It was true, nevertheless. They frittered away the spirituality of the Divine
Law, and its practical bearings, and still held on to those
forms and ceremonies which were instituted only to symbolise and represent it, hence making, as Jesus said, "His Father's house a den of thieves." They held on to the form
whilst the spirit had gone. They were making "Clean the
outside of the platter, while inside it was full of rottenness
and dead men's bones." And, dear friends, all corpses are
very much alike, when the spirit is gone out of them — one
is found to be about as good as another.

Alas! there is this tendency still in our fallen human
nature. It is so much easier, or satan makes it look so much
easier, to an unregenerate man, to rest in a form than to seek
till he finds the spiritual grace which that form represents.
That is to say, it is so much easier for an unregenerate man
to be circumcised or to be baptized, as the case may be, to
partake of the Lord's Supper, to keep outwardly the Sabbath
Day, to abstain from acts of immorality and open sin, and
to be decently moral and religious — all this he can understand and do for himself, and it looks to him so much easier,

and so it is, in the first instance, than bringing his evil, unregenerate heart to God for Him to circumcise it, and write His law in it, as he promises to do under the new covenant.

Now, that is what God wants every man to do. He wants him to bring this *heart to Him*, and let *Him renew it*. He says, "I will circumcise your hearts to keep my law." But, no! the unregenerate man rests in the outward form. He will not be at the trouble to sacrifice his idols, and cry mightily unto God. He will not seek until he attains the fulfilment of these promises; so he sits down and rests in the form.

Alas! alas! how many thousands in this so-called Christian land of ours to-day are just there. They have got the form; they are like the Jews — they are Pharisees with a Christian creed instead of a Jewish, the same in CHARACTER, only different in name. That is all the difference, hanging on to the creed of Jesus Christ, while they know nothing of its spirit, the form without the power; and then deny their professed Lord every day. Oh! are there any of this class here? My friend, my friend, if you never find it out until you come to die, you will find it out then, but it may be too late. May God, the Holy Spirit, help you to find it out this day, and bring that unrenewed, unrepentant, evil heart of yours to the Cross; bring it to God, and wait, and weep, if need be, and struggle, and knock, and cry, as He tells you, until He does renew it and write His law in it; then the outward form will be the expression of the inward grace. Then the fruit will be good, because it springs from a good root inside. The Lord help you!

This tendency to rest in form is just as great as ever, and, instead of putting away their idols, and bringing their conscience to be cleansed and kept clean by the precious blood, prayerfully and carefully walking before God, striving in all things to please Him, people get an outside form, but LIVE just like the world around them, calling Jesus, "Lord Lord," but not doing the things that He says. Now, I say that a pure Gospel requires that we bring our evil HEARTS to God to be renewed, and that we resolutely put away our idols, and that we wait on Him by the Cross until He renews our motives, tempers, tendencies, feelings, and dispositions, and makes us new creatures in Christ Jesus. Instead of doing this, people go on being circumcised or baptized, as the Jews did, and they call themselves "Israel," as they did; whereas, of the spiritual Israel they are utterly ignorant. They are the children of Hagar (as Paul says), and not the children of the promise. May the Lord help you to come and be made children of the promise!

Now, as in the individual, there is such a tendency to rest in form, so in the church collectively, hence this tendency to a formal religion. Just as it was with the Jews — their Temple service and the paraphernalia of Judaism — was all in all to them, and they thought that Jesus Christ was the most awfully severe and uncharitable person who ever appeared on the face of the earth, because He told them the truth. And the same class of character presents the same attitude now. We shall see when we get to the Judgment-seat of Christ which is the true charity — that which covers up things, or that which tears off the bandages, and shows people their hypocrisy, and, as we have just read, reveals to them the secrets of their hearts. I fear that we are very largely in the same condition as the Jews were when Christ came. I say "very largely," for I know that there are grand and glorious exceptions; but I speak of the great whole, and I am backed up in this opinion by some of the most thoughtful and spiritual men of this age. It is the lamentation everywhere — this formality and death. It reaches us from all parts of the land, yea, from all parts of all lands. I once heard a great divine, a leader of spiritual thought in his day, who has recently passed to heaven, say, "I consider that the writings of the Prophets are far more applicable to the state of the churches now than the writings of the New Testament, for we are in the same lapsed and fallen condition, as churches, as Israel of old was." So many think, and so many teach.

If this be the case, WHAT IS TO BE DONE? What would strike you should be done in this state of comparative — spiritual eclipse? Evidently it would be madness to *go on as we are.* That will mend nothing! Somebody must strike and do something worthy of the emergency. "There is no improving the future, without disturbing the present," and the difficulty is to get people to be willing to be disturbed! We are so conservative by nature — especially some of us. We have such a rooted dislike to have anything rooted up, disturbed, or knocked down. It is as much the work of God, however, to "knock down and pull up, and to destroy," as to build up, and God's real ambassadors frequently have to do as much of one as of the other. This is not pleasant work; but what is *necessary* to be done? Is it not manifestly necessary that we should go back to the simplicity and SPIRITUALITY of the Gospel, and to the early modes of propagating it amongst men?

In the two last discourses we tried to show what was the pure Gospel — calling men to forsake their sins, to cast away their idols, come out from the world of the ungodly and be separate in order that their sins might be forgiven, and that God might receive them, and they become

His sons and His daughters.   In the last we spoke of faith
and what it would do for us.

Now, with respect to the outward manifestations and
propagation of the Gospel, it is equally necessary to go back.
We have such a heap of rubbish to carry away — the ac-
cumulated traditionalism of ages to go through and dig
under — that it sometimes takes a considerable amount of
time, and force of character, and a great deal of the Spirit
of God, to enable us to do it.   Nevertheless, it must be done
if we are to reach a better state of things.

It seems to me, in order to do this we should not shrink
from a recognition of our lapsed and fallen condition.   That
was what the Jews did at the teaching of Jesus.   They
would not have His reproach.   They would not have the
light because it condemned them.   They rejected it.   They
persisted they were the children of Abraham — the children
of the promise.   They persisted they were all right, and
they pointed to the Temple and to their ceremonialism as a
proof of it; they would not have His testimony, would not
admit that they were wrong.   Do not let us imitate them.
Let us recognise this state of things.   Let us look it fairly
in the face.   Honesty is always the best policy both in
spiritual and in temporal things.   There is nothing gained
by ignoring a disagreeable truth.   It is best to face it.
Now there it is, and the best way is to hail any ray of light
that comes to us from any part of the heavens, even though
a carpenter should bring it, as He brought it to them — or a
fisherman, or a woman.   Never mind — let us hail the light
and apply it to ourselves.   Let us bring our hearts and
lives out into its blaze, and examine them by it, and improve
it to our own salvation and to the salvation of others.   If
the Jews had done that they would have been saved and

their nation. "Oh, if thou hadst known, even in this thy day,—this twelfth hour of the last day—the things that belong unto thy peace, but now, because of thy obstinate rejection, they are hid from thine eyes!" The Lord help us to take the light home to ourselves, each one.

We have seen that it is clearly laid down in the texts I have read that the law of adaptation is the only law laid down in the New Testament with respect to modes and measures. I challenge anybody to find me any other. While the Gospel message is laid down with unerring accuracy, we are left at perfect freedom to adapt our measures and modes of bringing it to bear upon men to the circumstances, times, and conditions in which we live—free as air. "I became all things to all men." The great Apostle of the Gentiles who had thrown off the paraphernalia of Judaism years before, yet became as a Jew that he might win the Jews. The great, strong intellect became as a weak man that he might win the weak. He conformed himself to the conditions and circumstances of his hearers, in all lawful things, that he might win them; he let no mere conventionalities, or ideas of propriety, stand in his way when it was necessary to abandon them. He suffered his limbs to be thrust into a basket, and himself let down over the wall, when necessary, for the success of his work. He who was brave as a lion, and hailed a crown of martyrdom like a conquering hero, as he was, yet was willing to submit to anything when the requirements of his mission rendered it necessary. He adapted himself to the circumstances. He was instant in season and out of season. Oh! what a hue-and-cry there is about out of season Christianity; "of some making a difference"—pulling them out of the fire by the hair of the head, if needful,—never mind—*save them*, SAVE

THEM. That is the great desideratum. Save them — pulling them out of the fire. Adapt your measures to your circumstances and to the necessities of the times in which you live. Now here it seems to me that the church — I speak universally — has made a grand mistake, the same old mistake which we are so prone to fall into of exalting the traditions of the elders into the same importance and authority as the Word of God, as the clearly laid down principles of the New Testament.

People contend that we must have quiet, proper, decorous services. WHERE IS YOUR AUTHORITY FOR THIS ? Not here. I defy any man to show it. I have a great deal more authority in this book for such a lively, gushing, spontaneous, and what you call disorderly service, as the Army services sometimes are, in this 14th of Corinthians, than you can find for yours. The best insight we get into the internal working of a religious service in Apostolic times is in this chapter, and I ask you — is it anything like the ordinary services of to-day ? Can the utmost stretch of ingenuity make it into anything like them ? But that, even, is not complete. We cannot get the order of a single service from the New Testament, nor can we get the form of a single church government. Hence one denomination think theirs is the best form, and another theirs; so Christendom has been divided into so many camps ever since; but this very quarrelling shows the impossibility of getting from the New Testament the routine, the order, and the fashion of mere modes. They cannot get it, because it is not there ! ! Do you think God had no purpose in this omission ? The form, modes, and measures are not laid down as in the Old Testament dispensation. There is nothing of this stereotyped routinism in the New Testament. Why ? Now there may be some who may have difficulties in this matter. I said to a gentleman, who came to me with this and that difficulty about our modes and measures, "I will meet your difficulties by bringing them face to face with the bare principles of the New Testament. If I cannot substantiate and defend them by that I will give them up for ever. I am not wedded to any forms and measures. To many of them I have been driven by the necessities of the case. God has driven me to them as at the point of the bayonet, as well as led me by the pillar of cloud, and when I have brought my reluctance and all my own conventional notions, in which I was brought up like other people, face to face with the naked bare principles of the New Testament, I have not found anything to stand upon! I find things here far more extravagant and extreme, than anything we do—looked at carefully." Here is the principle laid down that you are to adapt your measures to the necessity of the people to whom you minister; you are to take the Gospel to them in such modes and habitudes of thought and expression and circumstances as will gain for it from them a HEARING. You are to speak in other tongues — go and preach it to them in such a way as they will look at it and listen to it! Oh! in that lesson we read what beautiful scope and freedom from all set forms and formula there was. What freedom for the gushing freshness, enthusiasm, and love of those new converts! What scope for the different manifestations of the same spirit! Everything was not cut and dried. Everything was not prearranged. It was left to the operation of the spirit, and the argument that this has been abused is no argument against it, for then you might argue against every privilege. Here is abundant evidence that these new converts, each one, had the opportunity to witness for Jesus, opportunity and scope to give forth the gushing utterance of his soul, and tell otL er people how he got saved, or the experience the Holy Ghost had wrought in him. And look at the result! "If those that are unlearned, or unbelievers, come in, they are convinced of all, judged of all; and thus the secrets of their hearts are made manifest, and *falling down on their faces,* they will worship God, and report that God is in you of a truth." What unkind things have been said of the Salvation Army because people have fallen on their faces under the convicting power of the Spirit at our meetings; but you see this is Apostolic! And, oh, friends, what a glorious service this would be! You say it would look so strange. More the pity. More the pity that this natural, easy, domestic, familiar kind of testimony and witnessing of divine things should have become strange. May it not be because the experience which promoted it has become strange? May it not be that there is no more desire to testify because there is little to testify about? May it not be that there is want of the utterance of the Holy Spirit through the tongue because there is less of it in the soul? Oh! then, should we not make haste back to those days of simplicity and power? Should we not pray to be set free from the traditionalism and routinism in which Satan has succeeded in lulling us to sleep? I ask any saved man — Do you not remember the gushing love and enthusiasm of your first-found liberty? how you longed to tell everybody, and if you had been placed in such circumstances as these Corinthian converts, how gladly you would have testified to what Jesus had done for you. It was only the repressing, keeping down, and ultimately, I am afraid, the all-but extinguishing of the Holy Spirit's urgings that has led to the state in which many of you now are, and also the dead way in which many of our services are conducted.

Now let us look fairly at these things. I maintain that the only qualification — the only indispensable qualification — for witnessing for Christ, is the Holy Ghost. Paul, expressly, over and over again, abjures all merely human equipment. He expressly declares that these things were not the power, even when they existed, but that it was the Holy Ghost. Therefore, give me man, woman, or child with the Holy Ghost, full of love and zeal for God, and I say it is a great strength and joy to that convert to testify to the church and to the world, and it is the bounden duty of the church to give him the opportunity to do so. The Lord is going to demonstrate in this land, that He is not going to evangelize it by finished sermons and disquisitions, but by the simple *testimony of people saved from sin and the devil, by His power and His grace.* He is going to do it by WITNESSING, as He began.

Now I say, read your New Testament on this point, and you will be struck with the amazing amount of evidence for this unconventional kind of service. The world wants some more PENTECOSTS, — when Peters and Marys shall be so filled with the Spirit that they cannot help telling what God has done for them — male and female, men, women, and children — like the woman of Samaria, who, when she had found Him of whom Moses and the Prophets wrote, went and fetched her fellow-townsmen and women to hear Him. He wishes you to do the same, and this is the way the Lord is going to gather out His great and glorious kingdom in these latter days by the power of testimony in the Holy Ghost. He only wants witnesses to be able to go and say, " We speak that we do know " — *that* is the qualification. The Lord is multiplying such witnesses. Bless His holy Name.

But you may say — what did the Master Himself do?

Well, he adopted these very measures. I was so struck with this, when someone said, "Why, you are sending people to preach who cannot read or write!" For a moment I was staggered, but I asked him, "How many of the Apostles do you suppose could read and write when they were first sent out?" And then it was the questioner's turn to be staggered. There is no reason to suppose, with but two or three exceptions, that any of them could. Education then was far more uncommon than now. It was not reading and writing that was the great qualification for preaching Christ; it was KNOWING AND SEEING? It was not the power of eloquence, it was being able to cast out devils; that was the test. Give me somebody able to cast out devils, and I don't care whether they can read or write, or put a grammatical sentence together. That is of no consequence whatever. Why did not Jesus Christ call the doctors and scribes of His day? There were plenty of them — highly educated men with trained and disciplined minds. He was amongst them in the Temple, when He was twelve years old. He knew them. How was it he did not select these? He who could have commanded a legion of angels, could surely have commanded a few scribes and doctors to go to preach the Gospel. Why not? He acted on the law of adaptation. He wanted His Gospel preached to the great masses — not to the select few. Not to the educated "upper ten," but to the great masses of mankind. How was he to have his Gospel so preached, but by men like unto themselves? They fled from the educated doctors. They would not listen to the doctors, and they will not now. It may be very wicked, and obstinate and foolish, but such is the fact — they never have and they never will. Hence, Jesus Christ, instead of working a miracle, which he never did when it was unnecessary, chose the weak things of the earth to confound the mighty. He would, in the other case, have had first to have untaught all those scribes and doctors almost all they had learned. He would have had to set them free from the bonds of traditionalism. He would have had to remould their minds, and then equip them. There was no necessity for this when He found the fishermen ready to His hand. They were just the men He wanted. They only required tempering with the Holy Ghost, and they were ready for the work. They thought as the people thought; they spoke with and associated with the people, and, in fact, were of them. As he wanted the masses of men evangelized, he chose men from amongst the masses to evangelize them. Here was infinite wisdom. " I thank Thee, oh, Father, that Thou hast hid these things from the wise and prudent, and hast revealed them unto babes. Even so, Father, for so it seemed good in Thy sight." But he had a purpose in it, and the purpose was this — that the Gospel might be propagated in all climes and conditions of men, through any kind of an agent — Greek, Jew, Barbarian, Scythian, man, woman, child. Any person who has experienced its power in their souls may go and speak it to anybody they can get to hear them and everywhere! We are free as air and sunlight as to our choice of agencies, and it is time the Church woke up to this. The Lord have mercy on us! Is there not work enough to do? It makes my ears tingle and burn with shame when I hear people saying, " You must not send agencies here and there, and we can't have our organization interfered with." I say, " Are all the sinners converted in your neighbourhood?" Nay; has every poor, lost, wretched soul heard the name of Jesus, and the testimony of His Gospel? Are there not teeming thousands round about you who never heard His name, and who care nothing for Him, who live every day trampling His law under their feet? *For Christ's sake, send somebody after them.* If they will not have your doctors of divinity and your polished divines, get hold of fishermen and costermongers and send them! Let the people have a chance for their souls. Let them hear, for if they hear not, how shall they believe? Oh, they are dying for lack of knowledge — they are, friends; thousands are dying for the lack of knowledge. It is quite a common thing for us to get people into our services who say, "I never knew there was anything so pretty as that in the Bible. I didn't know you were reading from the Bible. We never heard anything like that before." Hundreds of men in this country were never in a place of worship, save to be christened or to be married, and a good many, sad to say, are living without being married. While we have been standing UPON OUR DIGNITY, WHOLE GENERATIONS HAVE GONE TO HELL! — if the Bible is true. How much longer shall we stand there? If Jesus had stood upon His dignity He would never have come to die between two thieves. The whole work of redemption is a work of humiliation, self-sacrifice and suffering; and if we are not willing to follow Him in that, we may as well give up professing His name.

The Lord help us to go down, down amongst the fishermen, amongst the poor, the weak, the unlearned, the vulgar, to "condescend to men of low estate."

ASSURANCE OF SALVATION.

"For what the Law could not do, in that it was weak through the flesh. God sending His own Son in the likeness of sinful flesh, and for sin, condemned sin in the flesh : That the righteousness of the Law might be fulfilled in us, who walk not after the flesh, but after the Spirit."—ROM. viii. 3, 4.

I will try, by God's grace, as much as in me lies, to deal with this subject in a way that shall not provoke controversy. I do deplore this. I wish there was a way of improving the future without disturbing the present, but it is a misfortune, I suppose, that there is not, and, however carefully we may guard ourselves in trying to lead the Lord's people higher, there is always somebody who will quibble and make objections and take exceptions. But we cannot help this. We must be true to our convictions of God's truth, and to what He has taught us, and revealed to us by His Spirit, for we speak the things that we do know, and do see, and do handle, of the Word of Life. However, I will try to keep to ground on which I think all really spiritual people will be agreed. And, oh! may the Holy Spirit give us one mind and help us to see in His light, and if there is anything we do not see in His light, oh! that this very hour He may show it to us, for He knows that we are all willing to see, and only longing and desiring to know the whole truth, as it is in Jesus. Let every sincere soul put up this prayer for himself and for me, as I put it up for myself and for you, that the Holy Spirit may lead us into all truth, at any rate as far as it is important to our own salvation and our practical exhibition of the salvation of Christ to other people, for a dying world is hanging upon our skirts. They are looking at us to find out what religion is. They will not come to this Book. They will not even hear about it, but they are looking to us to find it out: how momentously important it is that we should be truly living epistles, known and read of all men. We *are* epistles, whatever sort of doctrine our lives teach. We cannot help ourselves, for while we profess to be the Lord's, we are living epistles, known and read of all men.

Specially, then, I want first to look at the 3rd verse of the 8th chapter. Now, I thought it would, perhaps, be the most profitable way to look at this and meet the experience of some who I know are here, by trying to answer the question —

Wherein does the law fail to save us? Then we shall be able to see *wherein and how Jesus Christ transcends the Law.*

First, then, the Law does not fail in giving a knowledge of sin, for it is by the Law, as the Apostle says, that I know sin. Without the Law I was dead, so dead in sin that I did not realize it at all. Its power was so complete over me that I did not realize it was sin, and, therefore, was asleep and comparatively happy, but when the commandment came, "sin revived and I died" — that is, to all hope of making myself righteous. The commandment showed me the awful chasm there was between me and it. The Holy Commandment, just and pure and good — and myself unholy, impure, and unrighteous. A light flashed upon it, and I died in despair and utter helplessness. Thus, I say, the Law does not fail in giving knowledge of sin, for it is by the Law that I *get* the knowledge of sin.

Secondly, — Neither does the Law fail in begetting a sense of guilt and condemnation on account of sin, for it is by the Law again that I get this. I not only get the knowledge of sin by the Law, but I get the sense of guilt and condemnation for sin by the Law, for the Law comes in and condemus me. It is the spirit of death and condemnation to me : it says, " You should have done this, and because you have not done it you shall die." I feel that the Law is just and good, and yet I feel that I do not keep it, and, therefore, I have the sentence of condemnation upon me because I do not keep it. Then the Law does not fail in begetting a sense of condemnation and guilt on account of sin.

Thirdly, — Neither does the Law fail in producing *desire after righteousness and effort to attain it.* The Law begets in me the desire after righteousness, by contrasting my condition with the purity and holiness of God's Law. I see the Law to be good and holy, I see it to be desirable, and I desire to attain the righteousness of the Law. I am speaking now of a convicted sinner, as the Apostle did when speaking of the same character. A convicted sinner sees the righteousness and beauty of the Law of God. He sees that it is holy, just, and good. He sees that it is intended to make him holy, just, and good, for the Law is not sin, as the Apostle says, but is ordained unto righteousness, but the sinner has failed to attain it because of weakness, but he struggles to attain it. The first thing is to set himself to strive to attain the righteousness of the Law by his own efforts. This was the case with the Apostle. He longed to do what he could not, and he constantly did what he would not, and, as it was with the Apostle, so it is with every convicted sinner on earth. We were constantly longing after righteousness. We could not help looking on the beautiful, pure, and holy law of God, and we longed to keep it, and tried again and again until we were tripped down again and again, and died in utter despair, never being able to attain it for ourselves and of ourselves. So you see the Law begets first a knowledge of sin; secondly, it begets guilt and condemnation on account of sin; and, thirdly, desire after righteousness and effort to obtain it.

Thus far I think we must all be agreed. Wherein does the Law fail? It does all this for me. It brings me right up, as it were, — my schoolmaster lashing me right up to the cross, opening my eyes, creating intense desire after holiness and efforts for it, — and then it just fails me. Where? *At the vital point.* It cannot give me *power.* That is where the Law fails. It cannot give me power to fulfil itself. I am strengthless through the weakness of the flesh and the sinfulness of my nature to keep it, and so I struggle and wrestle for power to keep it, but I have not power. "What the Law could not do, in that it was weak, God sent His Son to do," and I maintain HE DOES IT, and *that* is the one vital point where *the Son transcends the Law.*

But there is a Gospel now-a-days, a Law-Gospel. A great deal of the Gospel of these days never gets any further than the Law, and some people tell me that it is never intended to do so, and then I ask, Wherein does Christ Jesus advantage me? What am I better for such a Gospel if my Gospel cannot deliver me from the power of sin? If through the Gospel I cannot get deliverance from this "I-would-if-I-could" religion, this "Oh!-wretched-man-that-I-am" religion, wherein am I benefitted by it? Wherein does your Gospel do more for me than the Law? The law convinced me of sin and set me desiring and longing after righteousness, but wherein is the superiority of Jesus Christ if He cannot lead me further than that? And I say, very well; your faith is vain, and Christ died in vain, and you are yet in your sins if that is all it can do. If that is all Jesus Christ can do, His coming is vain, and I am yet in my sins and doomed to hug this dead corpse to the last, and go down to hell, for death will never do for me what the blood and sacrifice of Jesus Christ cannot do for me. If Christ cannot supersede the Law then I am lost, and lost forever. Wherein, then, does this "Oh!-wretched-man" Gospel supersede the Law? Will anybody point it out to me?

Oh! but the *real* Gospel does. The Gospel that represents Jesus Christ, not as a system of truth to be received into the mind like I should receive a system of philosophy, or astronomy, but it represents Him as a REAL, LIVING, MIGHTY Saviour, ABLE TO SAVE ME *now*.

I said to a lady once, who was seeking this deliverance and who was struggling and wrestling, as I kneeled by her side, — "Wait a minute. Suppose Jesus Christ were here in His flesh, as He once was. Suppose he was to come to your side now, and put His hand upon you and say, 'Hush! I know your desire; I see your heart; I know what you are longing after. You are longing to be delivered from everything that grieves Me, upon which My pure eyes cannot look with allowance. You are wanting to be brought into full conformity to My will, and that is what I have come to do now. I have come to live with you. I am taking up my abode under this roof, and I will never leave your side. I will be with you by day and I will be with you by night. I will sit at the dinner-table and at the tea-table with you, and walk out with you, and go to bed with you, and rise up with you. Don't be troubled. I will never leave you and never forsake you.' Do you think if He were to come and say that, you would be able to trust Him?"

"Oh! yes."

"You would not be afraid?"

"Oh! no."

"Now, what would it be that would save you? Would it be the bodily presence of Jesus, which they laid in the sepulchre and which was as dead and helpless as any other clay when the spirit was gone out of it? No. It would be His spiritual presence, would it not? and His spiritual eyes seeing you, and His spiritual tongue speaking to you?"

"Yes."

"Well, then, this is just the presence that He has promised to be with everyone of His people, and now He is here and able to do this, and will abide with you and enable you to abide in Him if you will just trust Him. Now, just trust Him." And the Lord, by His blessed Spirit, did take and reveal this truth unto her, and just then and there she did leap into the arms of her Saviour and realize that He did save her.

Oh! friends, some people think we do not make enough of Christ. We make *all* of Christ; only it is a living Christ instead of a dead one. It is Christ in us as well as for us. We believe in Christ for us, and we should not have been here at all but for Christ for us up there for ever and ever, and no one will hasten to throw the crown at His feet readier than I shall; but we believe in order to do it we must have Him in us, and if He is not in us, then it is sounding brass and tinkling cymbal to call upon Him for us. He must be in us. Christ in us as well as for us, and those whom He is not *in* He will not be *for*. If He dwell not in you, ye are reprobates. But Christ in us, — an ever-loving, ever-present, Almighty Saviour, is just able to do what the angels said He should do, that for which He was called Jesus, to save His people from their sin.

Then how does He do this ? Wherein does he supersede the Law ? Wherein does Christ do for me and is made to me what the Law could not do ? We have seen what the Law could do and how far it could go. Now we see it fails just at the vital point of power. Now, how does Christ become this power to me ? How is He made unto me — not for me — up in Heaven (He is there, too), but how is He made unto me down here — wisdom, righteousness, sanctification, and redemption ? How does He deliver the people from their sins ? How does He save us from the power of sin ? Now, you who are longing to get free, try and listen to me, and oh ! *may the Holy Ghost teach us!*

He does this first by giving

Assurance of salvation. He saves and then He makes us conscious of the fact, which the Law could not do. All it could do was to set us struggling after it. It could not give us assurance. Now, by assurance, I mean the personal realization of my acceptance in Christ; my acceptance by the Father; my present acceptance — I mean the inward assurance which men and women find for themselves, or have revealed in themselves, which they know as a matter of consciousness. Not that which their minister tells them; not that which they learn from books, not that even which the Bible tells them only, for there are thousands of people who read the Bible who are not saved, and who know they are not. You all know there are thousands of people who believe it in vain.

I was walking down the anxious room at one of Mr. Moody's meetings, when two ladies came and said —

"Will you please speak to us?"

I don't know why they came to me, except it was my plain dress which made them think I ought to know, even if I did not, how to deal with souls. We took three chairs and sat down. The youngest was a lady about 30 or 33, and very intelligent, evidently an educated person, and the elder was an old lady, gorgeously attired. They sat down; and as to the younger one, there was no mistake about her earnestness. Mr. Moody had been preaching on "The Cities of Refuge," and showing how the soul who desired to to be saved had nothing to do and nothing to suffer, but only to run into the Cities of Refuge and be saved—a beautiful sermon for *convicted* sinners—and this lady said to me, almost passionately,—"How is it? there must be something wrong somewhere; there must be a mistake somewhere. I believe all that Mr. Moody has been saying, every word of it. I have believed every word since I was a little girl; in fact, I believe the whole of the New Testament—all about Jesus Christ, and I believe, moreover, that He died for me, and that He makes intercession for me, and yet I'm not saved a bit. I have no more power over sin than other people, and I know I am not saved. Now, what can be the reason? I am afraid it is want of faith."

That is the universal resort to fall back upon by all souls in that condition. I said,—"Will you be honest with me? It is of no use coming to a spiritual doctor any more than to a physical doctor if you are not frank; you would only mislead him. If you really want to be saved, be honest with me, and I will try, by the help of the Spirit, to help you."

"I do indeed want to be saved," she said. "I often go into my room, and weep and struggle, and pray for hours.

I try to believe. I think I have believed, and I come out and I am no better."

"Oh," I said to myself, "alas! here is the experience of thousands." "Tell me, in these times when you say you go into your room, and struggle, and pray, and strive, and believe; tell me, is there anything that comes up before the eye of your soul as an obstacle and difficulty that has to be put away or embraced; anything that comes up and that the Spirit of God says 'you must sacrifice this, or cut off that, or do the other?' Just tell me that."

She was quiet for a moment and speechless. She waited; then she drew her breath and said—"Well, yes, I am afraid there is."

"Ah!" I said, "that is it; it is not want of faith, it is want of obedience. Now you may go on another ten years, going into your room, struggling and striving, and until you trample that under your feet and say, 'Lord, I will follow Thee at all costs,' you will not be able to believe. I don't want you to tell me what it is; sufficient that you know it, and that the Lord knows it; but, after an experience of dealing with hundreds of souls just at this point, I tell you: you must give that up or embrace it, whatever it may be; I believe that is the cause of your trouble."

"Then," she said, "I will make no secret of it. I am the only member of an unconverted family that has any desire after God. My husband is a worldly, unconverted man, and I am in a worldly, unconverted circle, and always when I come to the Lord Jesus it comes up before me that I will have to confess Him and to live like a Christian, and I am not willing to do so."

"Then, my dear lady, it is the old story over again of the young ruler. Now, you know, I should be untrue to your soul if I were to go on plastering you with untempered mortar. There you are, make your choice. You cannot be a Christian, and not confess Christ. You cannot be a Christian, and not live like one before your unconverted relatives, and, therefore, if you are not willing to take up the cross and follow Him, you cannot become His disciple."

Then I went down on my knees with her, and we talked and prayed, and, at last, she said, —

"By the grace of God, I will confess Him."

Bless the Lord! and the light of salvation soon gladdened her eye, for it shone through her face. She found herself able to believe at once, and this is just the condition of thousands of souls. She got assurance then. She got saved. Before, she had been trying to believe she was saved, when she was not — quite a different thing to getting saved and then knowing it. People are told to believe this, that, and the other. As a gentleman said, at whose house I once stayed —

"I had a curious episode the other morning. I have had a gentleman here, of some note in the evangelistic world, for two or three days, and he came in the other morning at breakfast time and said, 'I am happy to tell you that both your gardeners are converted.' I was very thankful to hear it; and surprised that the work had been so quickly and thoroughly done. Well, I was walking in the grounds, and saw one of the gardeners. 'John,' I said, 'I am glad to hear the happy news.' He didn't seem to know what I meant.

"'What news, sir?'

"'Well, I hear you have given your heart to God this morning. You are converted, saved?'

"'Well,' John said, 'I could hardly say that, sir.'

"'Then what has happened? Something has happened in your experience — some change taken place?'

" 'Well,' he said, 'I don't hardly know that. The gentleman brought a Bible to me and read two or three verses, and asked me if I believed, and talked very nicely to me, and asked me again if I believed; then I said I did, and then he said I was all right, but I can't say I feel any different.' "

Now, I am afraid there has been sadly too much of that. There is all the difference between believing the letter of the Word and knowing that you are saved. I say, that man was *not* saved — was he ? I say, the lady who spoke to me in the anxious room, was *not* saved — was she ? And I say there are, alas ! thousands to-day in just that position. They are not saved. They manifest it by their fruits. They confess it. They write it to me in their letters on the right hand and on the left. Members of churches ten, fifteen, and twenty years, some of them ministers of the Gospel, and yet they tell me they are NOT SAVED ! !

Thus, you see it is something more than the belief after all. It is something more than what my minister tells me, something more than what books tell me, and what the Bible tells me. It implies and includes this; but something more than this; yea, very much more. It is believing in a living, personal, and almighty Saviour, and believing in Him now, and *that* faith brings the realization. *The other brings nothing.* When people believe thus, the Spirit comes into their hearts, crying, "Abba, Father!" To them there is no condemnation. They have the witness of the Spirit' that they are in Christ Jesus. The Spirit of the Son comes into their hearts, crying, "Abba, Father!" and they know by demonstration, by inward consciousness, that they have passed from death unto life. You see there is all the difference between the means of salvation and salvation itself. The means of salvation is not salvation. The means only brings salvation. "Thy faith hath saved thee." "By faith are ye saved," and when you are saved by faith, then consciousness attests the fact. Your own spirit attests the fact, and God's Spirit attests the fact, and you know it beyond controversy. You have assurance, aud this is the first indispensable condition of power over sin, for while I remain unassured of my salvation, oh! what power the devil has over me. "Oh," he says, "you're not saved at all. What is the good of your standing out on this point, for you are not saved at all. You may as well go all the way. You are under the power of sin, and may as well remain there. You have not got the witness of your salvation, and, therefore, what is the use of standing here or there?" But when we have the witness of the Spirit in our souls of our acceptance with God, that he does now for Christ's sake pardon and receive us, what power it brings. This is what the old divines called assurance of faith, a conviction wrought in the soul by the Holy Ghost that Jesus Christ has given Himself for me, that God has accepted that offering in view of my sin and transgression, and for its sake, and its sake *only*, has justified me freely from all things by which I could not be justified by the Law of Moses, and that in Him God becomes my Father, and now accepts me and looks upon me well pleased—a conviction wrought in my soul by the Holy Spirit; for, as the Apostle says, "No man can call Jesus 'Lord' but by the Holy Ghost." There must be the spiritual realization of Him as Lord. Why, anybody can call Him "Lord." Tens of thousands of people call Him "Lord" now-a-days, whom nobody pretends have the Spirit. What did he mean? He must have meant spiritual revelation, knowing Jesus Christ as its salvation—its Lord, such as He was revealed to Thomas, when he said, "My Lord and my God!"—really knowing him, and to this the Holy Ghost alone can testify. Do not tell anybody they are saved. I never do. I leave that for the Holy Ghost to do. I tell them how to get saved. I try to help them to the way of faith. I will bring them up as close as ever I can to the blessed broken body of their Lord, and I will try to show them how willing He is to receive them, and I know that when really they do receive Him the Spirit of God will tell them quickly enough they are saved. He will not want any assistance about that. I have proved it in hundreds of cases. Nobody knows the soul but God. Nobody can see the secret windings of the depraved heart but God. Nobody can tell when a full surrender is made but God. Nobody can tell when the right hand is cut off, or the right eye plucked out, but God. Nobody can tell when a soul is whole-hearted but God, and as soon as He sees it, He will tell that soul it is saved; but, if God has not told you, be up and doing and strive to make your calling and election sure, for you are not saved yet, or you would know it. What are you to believe unto? Hope? Oh, dear no! you don't believe unto hope. Effort? Oh, no! you had that before in the Law. SALVATION? Yes! and if you believe unto *salvation* you will get *saved*, and if you are not saved you have never believed unto salvation. Instead of trying to make yourself happy in this state of uncertainty and misery, for Christ's sake, get up and get saved. It is a great deal easier to get saved than it is to make yourself believe you are saved when you are not. The one is a philosophical impossibility; the other is a glorious possibility at any moment when you get low enough before God, and give up all and take His Son as your precious and almighty Saviour. God's Gospel is beautifully adjusted to the laws of our mental constitution. He who wrote, framed, and conceived it, created us, and He has made it like a key to fit the lock, and knows just the conditions that are necessary, and He has conformed His Gospel to those conditions.

My friend, if you want to know you are saved, this is the only response I can give, and the only way I know, and I have talked to hundreds of souls of all grades and conditions, to many ministers of the Gospel, deacons and leaders, in just this state. For years my labors were exclusively carried on in churches and chapels, where, naturally, church members have come, and they have told me by hundreds with their own lips that they have been members so many years and were never saved. Now I am not, therefore, speaking without experience in this matter. I tell you when you believe in a Scriptural sense, you will get saved in a Scriptural sense. When you put out of your head all these new-fangled notions about faith, and cease to believe in any faith that does not save the soul and bring it into conscious union with Jesus Christ, and resolve to have it, then you will get it. I never knew a soul come to that in my life who did not get it. I have had people before me who were worn almost to skeletons and were driven almost mad, and the first thing they have said has been, when I have asked the reason, "Oh! I have no faith. It is want of faith!" This is the universal lament, and, when we have come to close quarters, I have invariably found it has been no such thing, but want of OBEDIENCE, which spiritual teachers have not had the wisdom to discern as Christ did in the heart of the young ruler, "Yet one thing thou lackest." He saw that young man's besetting sin was covetousness. I do not know that He would have said that to every rich man, but in the case of the young ruler He saw that the love of his possessions was so paramount that unless he let them go and made a clean sweep he could not follow Him and be a consistent disciple, and so He said, "Sell all, and come and follow Me," and the young man went away sorrowful; and, mark you, Jesus Christ did not call him back, and yet He looked after him and loved him. His great, benevolent heart panted after him, and He desired to have him; but He saw it would be a greater evil to call him back and compromise the conditions of salvation than to let him be lost. And yet, methinks, if there was any case in which a compromise could be made, it would have been in this. He did not do as many would have done in our day — called him back and said, "Here, young man, I think I have been a little too hard on you. You shall sell half, and keep the other half, and come and follow Me." Oh, no! Everybody would be saved at that rate. There would be no test of whole-hearted consecration to Him then. If you can let people into heaven on terms like these, they would be only too ready to close with them. But whether ministers teach people the truth or not, the Holy Ghost does; and He puts His finger on the sore spot, and says, "If you want to follow me, you will have to renounce this, and give up that, or embrace the other," and if the soul says, "No, Lord; I would follow, but suffer me first to go and hug this idol;" then Jesus Christ says, "Very well, go!" That is the sort of faith people are resting in.

I see we shall not get any further than assurance of salvation. You are panting after it. You are longing for it. You may have it. God wants every one of His people to have it. Get saved, and you will know it. Use your Heavenly Father's letter to find your way up to Him. It is not the letter you are to rest in: it is the God who wrote it. Use the letter to get at the Spirit, for the letter will not save you—it is the Spirit that saves you. Hug this volume to your heart as the expression of your Father's will and the record through which you are to believe on His Son, but it is the Son who is to save you. People talk about exalting Christ. I think this is His glory, that He can save His people and make them know it, and make them feel it, and carry them as He did Paul and Silas through the prison and the stocks, singing His praises and making them inexpressibly happy in His love. Assurance of Salvation! Everybody wants it when they come to die. Why don't people get it while they live? Did you ever know a professing Christian come to die who did not want it? Did you ever know one dare to die without it? and, if you ever did, you know what a miserable death it was. Then, I contend, what is necessary to die with, is necessary to live with. Why not get it while you live? Assurance! Assurance! And you can have it just now. Hallelujah! Amen.

HOW CHRIST TRANSCENDS THE LAW.

In answer to letters received since last Sabbath, I would just say that the writers tell me that they have been struggling for years for assurance; that they do receive the testimony of God concerning His Son; that they do believe that Jesus Christ died for their sins; still they have no peace or joy. I want you to mark well that assurance of salvation is the testimony of God's Spirit to a fact which has transpired, and if that fact has not transpired God's Spirit will never testify to it. You may think you believe; but, oh, I feel sure numbers of people are deluded here. They think they believe because they receive into their minds the written record that God has given of His Son; but they have not believed and rested on the promise in such a way as to bring the witness of the Spirit. They have stopped short of that. They have been satisfied with the letter.

Now, do not think that I underestimate the letter. Perhaps few of you, if any, value this Word more than I do, but I have known very few people who have rested merely in the letter (and I have known many), who, when I have come into close conversation with-them, have not been miserably dissatisfied, unassured, sin-conquered souls; and that fact alone teaches me that there is something wrong. Now, that is not the glorious liberty of the children of God.   That is not knowing God in the scriptural sense.

Take God's way, and then the witnessing Spirit will come. Of course people are not assured because they have nothing to be assured of!   They have no salvation, and, therefore, they cannot be assured of it.   Get salvation and you will get assurance.   This is what you want.   IT IS FOR YOU. Here it is.   There is no other religion recognized in this Book.   All the saints to whom Paul wrote knew they were saved.   Here and there was an exception, where they had fallen back and got into bondage, as some of you have; but, as a rule, he recognizes the fact that they all were saved, were rejoicing in the assurance of it, and this is the normal condition of the children of God.   I do not say such a person may not occasionally slip.   He may occasionally.   He may lose his scroll, as Pilgrim did, but he cannot, will not rest till he finds it again!

Then you say, "I am not to believe, I suppose."   Oh, yes! you are.   Take the blessed record to your heart, but do not rest in the letter.   Go ON until you find the substance of things hoped for—the substance.   There is a substance in spiritual things quite as much as there is in natural things, and those who really and truly believe, know it.   No one can testify when you do really and truly believe but God's Spirit, for the things of a man knoweth no man save the spirit of a man that is in him, and just so with the things of God.   He searcheth the hearts and minds, and knows when you are sincere and real and true; and when you seek Him with all your heart you will find Him, and He will come and testify to that fact—and oh! if you have not this testimony, suspect yourself.   Do not throw discredit upon God.   Begin over again and get assurance.

Oh ! what POWER assurance of salvation gives ! when the individual can say I know ;—not merely I believe, but *I know*. Faith is the means to assurance, but assurance is not faith, and faith is not assurance.　Assurance is the result of faith, and when you have the right sort of faith you will have assurance, and until you get assurance do not trust yourself. Persevere until you get it.　God will never leave a sincere soul in the dark.　You must come down to the foot of the cross in the little children's way—give up all for Christ, and make up your mind that you will follow Him at all costs, and then cast your guilty soul upon His broken, bleeding sacrifice, and, as soon as you do this, God will send the answer of His Spirit.

But I want to go a little further in showing how Christ supersedes the Law.

We have noted in a former sermon that He does this, first, by giving assurance.

Secondly, I want to show, by giving POWER OVER SIN. Now we shall be safe here.　I trust this will not be controverted ground.　I believe He can do a great deal more for His people than this, but we will stop here this afternoon.　By-and-bye we may, perhaps, go further.　Christ gives His people power over sin.　Now, this is a necessity of our position. We have, as we have seen, been all slaves of sin.　Sin is, indeed, the sting of death.　Now, how is it if there is no deliverance from this dreadful plague and scourge of God's people—how is it that the Holy Ghost sets every real child of God struggling after it ?　Whatever may be a man's theory in his creed, you get him on his knees, and he will begin to pray to God to save him from sin.　Sin is the abominable thing which he hates, and longs to be delivered from ; and the universal experience of God's people is that the Spirit urges them to seek to be saved from sin. I have heard people argue powerfully against the possibility of being delivered from sin, and the next time I have heard them pray, they have asked God for the very same thing, and I have said, "Thank God, that is the Holy Ghost teaching him now; he cannot help praying for it, whether he believes in it or not." If I have been under the power of sin, so as to become its complete slave, and Jesus Christ comes and pardons me for the past, and delivers me from the guilt and condemnation which came upon me in consequence of the past, what do I want? I want some new power. I want something besides pardon. I want power, or I shall be down again the next minute.

What God does for us through Jesus Christ outside of us is one thing, and what He does in us by Jesus Christ is another thing, but the two are simultaneous, or one so immediately succeeds the other that we hardly discern the difference. Now, I say, I want power to enable me to meet that temptation which is coming on me to-morrow, as it came on me yesterday, and, if Jesus Christ pardons ever so, and leaves me under the reigning power of my old appetites, what has he done for me? I shall be down in the mud, and to-morrow night I shall be as great a sinner as ever. I want power. I want regeneratian—as the Holy Spirit has put it. I want the renewing of the spirit of my mind. I want to be created anew in Christ Jesus; "made a new creature."

Now, this is where Jesus Christ transcends the Law. The Law could not renew the spirit of my mind. It could only show me what a guilty rebel I was. It could not put a better spirit in me. It could not extract the venom, but only show it to me, and make me writhe on account of it. But Jesus Christ comes and does this for me—gives me power. How?

Now, I hope those friends who think that I do not suffi-
ciently exalt the Saviour, will mark this. How does He give
it to me? He unites me to Himself. I am dead to the Law.
He delivers me from the condemning power of the law when
He pardons me, and then He does not leave me there, but
He marries me to Himself. He unites me to another husband, and then I attain power to bring forth fruit unto God.
A beautiful—a wonderful figure! We may not pursue it;
but, oh! what a wonderful figure! Alone under the Law's
power, my old husband, I could do nothing but agonize,
wrestle, and desire. There was no power in me; but when
Jesus Christ comes and unites me to Himself, then He gives
me power to bring forth fruit unto God. It is by the UNION
OF MY SOUL WITH HIM. You say, "Explain it!" I
cannot. God Himself cannot explain it We cannot explain
it, but we know it. As Jesus said to Nicodemus: "The
wind bloweth where it listeth, and thou hearest the sound
thereof, but canst not tell whence it cometh, and whither it
goeth: so is every one that is born of the Spirit." The mys-
tery is too great to be explained, but there is the beautiful
illustration, united to Christ I have power to conquer, to subdue, to trample under foot those things which heretofore have
been my master, and by virtue of Him I retain the power,
and in no other way. Oh! dear friends, what a delusion there
is on the subject of Christian knowledge. If knowledge
could save people, what a wonderful world we should have
to-day!

Knowledge is as powerless as ignorance. A man is not a
whit nearer God, or more like Christ, because he has his head
crammed with this Word. In fact, some I have known who
have been best acquainted with the Word, have been the
greatest slaves of sin, and even ministers of Jesus Christ

have confessed to me that they have been bond-slaves of some besetting sin. It is not in knowledge, and God is raising up thousands of witnesses to this fact, that it is not in knowledge—it is in union with Him, and the little child in intellect and intelligence, who has the real vital union with Jesus, has more power in his little finger than the most eminent theologian has in his whole body without Christ. The things of God can only be understood by those who have the Spirit of God. The world by wisdom knows not God any more now than it did in days of old. The things of the Spirit are only spiritually comprehended. Hence this beautiful union cannot be explained, but I only know it is spoken of all through the Bible, both in the Old Testament and in the New, as knowing God. After God has summed up the failures of His people, He gives them a promise, and says, "I will betroth thee unto Me in righteousness for ever, and thou shalt KNOW the Lord," as though that were the end of the whole matter, coming really and truly to know Him. When they come to that living union of soul with Him, it brings the vital sap like the branch of the tree—another of his own beautiful illustrations. "Abide in me, and I in you. As the branch cannot bear fruit of itself, except it abide in the vine; no more can ye, except ye abide in me." You know what the branch is when it is broken off. It is a branch. It retains the form of a branch, and, for a while, the beauty and greenness of a branch, but it is broken off. There is no power in it. Suppose it could maintain that form. Alas! human branches often do, and maintain those green leaves fragrant in beauty, as it was when it was first lopped off. It can never bear fruit. Why? Because the communication is cut between itself and the vine, and there is no sap in the fibre. It is cut off. Now, my friends, you can see why a soul who has never been truly united to Christ in this living, spiritual marriage, cannot bear fruit unto God.

You can be like a branch. You can get so much scriptural knowledge that you can look just like a real Christian. Alas! You can get many of the feelings of a Christian, and of the sentiments, as well as a great many of the aspirations and desires of a Christian. You may be so like a branch that nobody but Jesus Christ may know you are not in that true Vine, and yet you have never, as the Apostle says, been grafted on to the olive tree. And therefore, you go on weeping, and struggling, and trying to perform the function of a living branch, when all the while you are a dead one. You go on trying to bring forth fruit unto God when the one indispensable condition of fruitfulness is wanting. You have got every other condition. You may even be nailed up to the wall close to the vine. You may be such a professor that nobody may ever doubt you. You may be so close to the vine than nobody can detect your want of union but the gardener who comes and closely inspects you, and yet you may not have one fibre circulating the real spiritual sap. HENCE YOU HAVE NO POWER, and down you go when the temptation comes. Ah! what weary years of strife some professing Christians have! they would be ashamed to tell, only death forces it from their lips before they die—trying to perform all the functions of living men when they have never been spiritually made alive. All they have ever had has been what Paul depicts as the struggle of a poor convicted sinner unable to bring forth any fruit unto God.

Now, you say this union with Him — what is it? Well, I cannot explain it. You, who know what it is, cannot explain it: so to know the Lord as to be conscious of the living sap circulating through your soul, anointing your eyes with eye-salve, giving you eyes to see, a voice to speak, feet to run, and hands to serve—making you in all a "new creature."

Now my dear friends, those of you who have not got this, never mind who comes to you and brings a Bible, and says, "Do you believe this and that, and if you do you are saved." Say " Miserable comforters are ye all : I will never be content until I know God."

I made up my mind to this when I was 15 years of age. I had had the strivings of God's Spirit all my life, since I was about two years old. My dear mother has often told me how she went up stairs to find me crying, and when she questioned me, I said I was crying because I had sinned against God. Thank the Lord, I do not say this boastingly. I have good cause to be ashamed that I was so long before I fully gave myself up: but all through my childhood I was graciously sheltered by a watchful mother from outward sin, and, in fact, brought up as a Christian. When I came to be between 15 and 16, when I believe, I was thoroughly converted, the great temptation of Satan to me was this : " You must not expect such a change as you read of in books. You have been half a Christian all your life. You always feared God. You must content yourself with this." Oh! how I was frightened! It must have been the Spirit of God that taught me. I was frightened at it. I said, "No, no." My heart is as bad as other people's, and if I have not sinned outwardly I have inwardly. I cried to God to show me the evil of my heart, and said, "I will never rest till I am thoroughly and truly changed, and know it, as any thief, or any great outward sinner." I went on seeking God in this way for six weeks, often till two o'clock in the morning, wrestling, and I told the Lord I would never give up, if I died in the search, until I found God, and I did find him, as every soul does, when it comes to him in that way. I cried for nothing on earth or in heaven, but that I might find Him whom my soul panted after, and I did find Him, and you can find Him. I knew Him. I can't tell how, but I knew Him. I knew He was well pleased with me. I knew that we held sweet converse often to the small hours of the morning together, and I know that I was as happy in His love, and far more happy than I ever was in any human love before or since.

Now, friends, you can all have this union. He is no respecter of persons. He has bought it for us. He saw our weakness. He contemplated our moral inability. He need not have come if we could have known God by the Law. If the old covenant had been perfect, there would have been no room for a second. It brought us not into the full realization and enjoyment of God, but the new covenant does. It cleanses the conscience from dead works to serve the living God, and God is henceforth revealed to his people, and they walk with Him. "If any man will do His will, I will come to him, and make My abode with him and My Father," and when a man has got the Father and Son, he is a match for satan and all his forces. Union with Christ!

Oh! do you think this is a mere allegory of the Apostle's? It is a beautiful illustration. When he delivers us from the condemning, reigning power of the Law, we become married to Jesus Christ. Then we get a power to produce in our affections, and hearts, and lives, and all about us — such things as God delights in.

Now, mark, all through the New Testament, and, indeed, the Bible, no truth is taught with greater force and frequency than this, that without a vital union of soul with Christ, all ceremonies, creeds, beliefs, professions, church ordinances, are sounding brass and tinkling cymbals, and all who trust in them will be deceived. This is the very essence of the Gospel. This is what He came for, and all (and, oh! how my heart bleeds to think and say it) who do not attain to this real vital union with Him will be *lost*. Everything else falls short of our need and the purpose and end of the Gospel of Christ.

He came on purpose for us to have this union with Himself. Circumcision, nor uncircumcision, nor anything else availeth anything but this faith, which worketh by love and brings the Spirit of Christ into our hearts. Oh! bear with me! Dear friends, have you got it? Have you got this vital union with Christ? Are you bringing forth fruit unto God? If not, I beseech you give up daubing yourselves with untempered mortar and trying to make yourself believe you are right when you are all wrong. However much desire, purpose, hope, aspiration, struggle, or whatever else you have, if you have not attained to this, you are not saved yet, and you are not in the kingdom.

In conclusion, bring forth fruit unto God, or, as the Apostle has it, "having your fruit unto holiness and the end eternal life"—and in another place, for the "end of the commandment, the purpose of the commandment, the ultimatum of the commandments is, charity, love out of a pure heart," and so in many other passages; but we just take these at random.

The result! What is the result? That we may bring forth fruit unto God. Jesus Christ in this union recognizes the fact that we are still in the body; still in the world; and that we are open to the attacks of Satan. He knows—has foreseen, and has provided for the temptations of the flesh—that is, the temptations which come to us through our natural appetites, and instincts, and desires, as they came to Him. He was hungry, and after enduring the great temptation in the wilderness. There was no sin in being hungry. He was intensely hungry, for He had nerves, and a brain, and a heart, as we have. He was a perfect man, and He suffered all the consequences of that lengthened strain upon His nervous system, and the Devil took advantage of the existence of that intensely excited condition of His body by tempting Him unlawfully to gratify it. For he said, "Command these stones that they be made bread." This was unlawful under the circumstances (we will not stop to explain why), and, therefore, He said, "Get thee behind me, Satan." He would rather suffer the hunger than unlawfully gratify it, and therefore, He did not commit sin. It matters not (and this will meet the case of some who have written to me) how intensely excited any physical appetite may be — that is not sin. The more you suffer through excitement of the physical appetite, whatever kind it may be, the more Jesus Christ sympathizes with you, for He was tempted in all points, like as we are, yet without sin, and if you endure unto blood He will sympathize with you more than with the man who does not have to endure and resist. You do not sin because of the appetite merely being excited. I think Satan gets some sincere souls to bring themselves into condemnation when God does not condemn them. If you resist as He did; if you say, "Get thee behind me, Satan," you sin not. What was Eve's sin? Unlawful self-gratification. The Devil might have tempted her until now, if she had lived so long; if she steadily resisted him she would not have brought sin into the world.

Under the law it is sin, and you struggle against it, but you have no power and down you go. United to Christ you see it is sin, and you have power, and you resist it, and the Devil runs away, and that is the difference. You are married to a new husband now, and he is more than a match for the old Devil. He is a conquered foe, while you abide in Christ. He can torment, harass, and excite you, stimulate your natural appetites, but he cannot make you sin while you abide in Christ. "Little children, keep yourselves from idols."

Then, again, we are open to the temptations of the world, but this is provided for. Jesus Christ knows that we are susceptible to the liking of nice things like other people, and great things, and ambitious schemes, and the world's praises and censures. God's people are only sadly too familiar with this, and the weak part of their nature would respond to it, and they would fall, but now they are united to Christ, He opens their eyes to see that it is Satan and the world. When the Devil takes them to the top of the pinnacle, and shows them all the glory of the world, he tries to make them think it would be very nice to have it; he tempts them to think it hard that they should be regarded as such paltry and mean people because they belong to Christ; but when they are throughly and truly united to Jesus, He gives them power to say as He did, "Get thee behind me, Satan," for it is written, "Thou shalt love the Lord thy God, and Him ONLY shalt thou serve"—not Him and the world. Oh! thank God, if you have got there. Praise the Lord if you understand that.

Then he comes not only through these avenues; but he comes again with direct, subtle, spiritual influence, with his old insinuation, as he came to Eve, and says, "Hath God said this and that?" He tries to inject doubts as to God's goodness and veracity into the believer's soul, as he used to do under the Law, and under the Law the convicted sinner's soul used to swell with rebellion, and say, "Yes, it is a hard case."

Satan comes and vomits these thoughts, and tries to excite these ill feelings and these chargings of God foolishly in the believer's soul, but by virtue of his union with Christ, who came not to do His own will, but His Father's, and who spoke only the things that his Father bade Him, the believer says, "Though He slay me yet will I trust Him, and shall not the Judge of all the earth do right?" and the Devil is gone. And then when the Devil is foiled at all these points, he tries higher ground. "Really you are a wonderful Christian—you are. You have had special grace, for surely very few people can have resisted the amount of temptation that you have. Really you must be one of God's specially favoured ones. Now cast yourself down. It is written, 'He shall give His angels charge concerning you.'" Spiritual presumption next. When he is foiled through the world, and the flesh, and the Devil, then he doffs his old robe and comes as an angel of light. But the soul's Bridegroom is hard by, and he says, "Be not ignorant of Satan's devices. Behold I am thy salvation. Trust, and be not afraid." And so the soul refuses to cast itself into unnecessary troubles, and is content to abide in and walk with its Lord. That is how He gives us the victory. He shows us Satan's devices, and gives us power. I cannot tell you how. We don't know how. We only know He gives it to us, and we only know that one instant separated from Him we fall and become as other men. We only know that in those seasons when our faith has relaxed its grip we have gone down in the mud and been overcome as others. It is by faith we stand, and while, like Peter, we keep our eye on Him, and hold Him fast, the waves may roar, and the winds may howl, but He holds us by virtue of this union, and we bring forth fruit unto God. We have power over the Devil. He said, "I will give you power over all the power of the enemy, and I will make you conquerors." This is the deliverance of the SAINTS. This is the life of the saints. This is the fight of faith. This is the SORT OF RELIGION THAT DOES TO DIE WITH ! ! !

People all over the land are astounded at our poor, weak, illiterate Salvation Army soldiers. A gentleman in a meeting on Easter Monday, a leading man of thought and experience in the holiness world, who was there all day—when my daughter said, " Why don't you speak ? " said, " One feels as if one can't speak in these meetings." " Why ? " These people have such unction from the Holy One that they are wiser than their teachers. Another gentleman, of considerable position, too, in the religious world, said, " I feel like getting down at their feet. I feel as if they could teach me." How is it that they have such power — those babes in intellect and intelligence ? All over the land people say this to me. People who talk and go ahead in other meetings, when they get into our meetings, say " I can't. They are so far ahead of me that, to tell you the truth, I have nothing to say." I say, the Lord have mercy upon you, and make haste and come up after them. Only get down from your high mightiness as low as these people, and you will get it. It is not because they are poor and illiterate that they have power, but because they are babes in spirit. Even as Christ said, " I thank thee, oh ! Father, that Thou hast hid these things from the wise and prudent, and hast revealed them unto babes." The simple spirit, the teachable believing soul—oh ! how much more it learns of God, in one hour's precious communion, than Doctors of Divinity learn in weeks of close study, who have not got it, because it is the SPIRIT that teaches the things of God. This is union with Jesus that bringeth forth fruit unto God, and oh ! the wonderful things it enables us to bring forth. If you would all follow me, as far as I have gone this afternoon, and make the resolution I made at 15 years of age, not to be put off with theories, but that you will KNOW THE LORD, that you will have this Divine union, and that you will never rest till you get it and know you have it. If we could all get thus far saved, what happiness there would be amongst you. There would be some Hallelujahs. Many of you would be surprised how you would find your tongues. A gentleman once said to me, "I never did shout in my life, but upon my word I couldn't help it." I said, "Amen. It's time, then, you began." I hope it may be the same with many of you. When the Lord comes to His Temple and fills it with His glory you won't know what to do. You must find vent somewhere, or you will be as the poor old negro said he was — "Ready to bust his waistcoat." We feel so about temporal things. People drop down dead with joy. People shriek with grief. People's hearts stand still with wonder at the news they have heard, perhaps from some prodigal boy. I heard of a mother, not long ago, whom some one injudiciously told of the sudden return of her son, who dropped down dead and never spoke. And when the Master comes to His Temple, that glorious blessed Holy Saviour, whom you profess to so long after and to love, and who has been absent so many years, and whom you have been seeking after with strong crying and tears, comes, do you think it will be too much to shout your song, or go on your face, or do any extravagant thing? Oh! no, if there is reality, you cannot help yourself. The manifestation will be according to your nature. One will fall down and weep in quietness, and the other will get up and shout and jump. You cannot help it. Like the two martyrs, one rejoiced in the realization of God's presence, and the other, who was in darkness, yet did not deny his Lord and turn his back upon Him. He continued in the way of obedience, and the other was encouraging him to hope and believe the Master would come; but He did not come until they started from the dungeon to the stake; so they fixed upon a sign, and the one said to the other, "If He comes you will give me the sign on the road." The Master did come, but the martyr could not confine himself to the sign. He shouted, raising his arms to his fellow martyr, "He's come, He's come, He's come!" He couldn't help it. When He comes you won't be ashamed who know it. When you really get a living Christ for your husband you will be more proud than the bride is who has got a husband worth being proud of, and you will love to acknowledge and praise Him, and the day is coming when you will crown Him before all the host of heaven. The Lord help you to accept Him, and put away everything that hinders His coming. Amen.

THE FRUITS OF UNION WITH CHRIST.

"That the righteousness of the Law might be fulfilled in us, who walk not after the flesh, but after the Spirit."—Rom. viii.; 4.

We dealt, on Sunday week, with "What the Law could not do;" and last Sabbath afternoon we dealt with "What Jesus Christ could do," by uniting us with Himself and giving us power. I want, this afternoon, to direct your attention to the fruits of this union — THE LAW FULFILLED IN US. What does it mean?

First. — I want just to say two or three words about Law in the abstract. There seems to me to be an awful misconception of the Apostle's writings respecting the Law, caused by "wresting" and misapplying what he says on justification by faith. People should bear in mind that much of this Epistle, and some others, was written on purpose to meet the extreme legal notions of the Jews, who had no other idea of righteousness than that of their own efforts to keep the Law (Romans ix. 3), and that, therefore, the Apostle was bound, as any other writer would be in such circumstances, to put the extreme view on the other side. Many, not considering this, separate these passages from their explanatory connections, and from all the rest of the Word of God, and preach now-a-days that we have nothing to do with the Law. Hence, there has come to be a spirit of Antinomianism abroad in the land, compared with which the Antinomianism of bygone ages was innocency itself. God helping me, I shall never cease to lift up my voice against it.

Now, please, first note that there is, in this writing, talking, and singing about the Law, a great deal of mental fog and confusion. People should be very careful, when they come to such matters as these, to be clear in their own minds as to what the Apostle is writing about; but I find frequently in such writings and songs a total misapprehension as to the meaning of the Apostle, and a total confounding of the Moral with the Ceremonial Law. Now, always mind, when you read anything about the Law, to examine and find out which Law is meant, whether it is the great Moral Law, which never has been, and never can be, abrogated, or the Ceremonial Law, which, in Christ, certainly was done away. Mind which, because your salvation may depend upon that point. If you make a mistake there you may be lost through it; therefore be very careful. Now, I say that people confound this, and, consequently, there is a perfect hodge-podge of theology in this day, which I defy anybody to understand. People do not know what they are to believe, or what they are not to believe. As a gentleman said, not long ago, "it is confusion confounded. I go to one meeting and hear this, and then I go to another meeting and hear that, and, very often in the very same meeting, the speakers will get up and flatly contradict each other!" "Exactly," I said, "but you have got the Bible. Why don't you study that for yourself? Why not use common sense — why not let your conscience speak?" "But," said he, "why do not our ministers do it?" "Because," said I, "many of them do not know it themselves. Let your conscience speak, and God will not let you go wrong." It is an honest heart people want, and then they will get the light. People sing about the Law, talk about the Law, and glory in being free from the Law, in a lawless, Antinomian spirit, as far from anything Paul ever wrote or meant as hell is from heaven! Oh, it is an awfully bad sign when people are out of love with the Law of God! David made his boast in the Law of his God, he meditated on it by day and by night, and its precepts were his delight; he loved it with all his soul, and so did David's Son, and he is too much in love with his Father's Law and Will, to hold fellowship with anybody who does not love it. As He said to the Jews, " He that is of God, heareth God's words; ye, therefore, hear them not, because ye are not of God;" and, again, of His disciples, "For I have given unto them the words which Thou gavest me." So, mind, if you do not love the words, the expression of the will of God, you do not love God, and if you do not love the Father neither do you love the Son. This is the very accusation which He brought against the Jews, that they had made void His Father's Law. Let us mind, then, the distinction always made between the great Moral and the Ceremonial Law.

In the second place: I want you to note, that when you have ascertained that the Apostle is speaking of the Moral Law — and he appears to speak disparagingly of it — he is always referring to its inability to justify a sinner, or to produce spiritual life. This, he says, it could not do; but he never speaks disparagingly of it as the guide and standard of spiritual life after it is given. No! he goes back to it as the only standard, and so did Jesus Christ. They continually refer to the Law as the highest expression of the holiness and righteousness of God, and as the standard by which we are to set our souls and consciences. What other standard have we but the Law? How am I to judge of my thoughts, words, and actions, but by the Law? Where has Jesus Christ given me any other guage? And if people would but read on, and let the Apostle explain himself, they would understand him better, and not get into such tanglements and mazes! Paul is most careful to guard himself against the Antinomian conclusions which he saw might be drawn from isolated parts of his writings. He says, "Do we, then, make void the Law through faith? nay, we establish the Law."

And, again, "Wherefore the Law is holy, and the commandment holy, just, and good;" and, again, when he says, that "To them that are without Law he became as without Law;" he guards himself by a parenthesis, "Being not without Law to God, but under the Law to Christ." That is, under the great universal Law of love, which fulfils all other law; for "Love is the fulfilling of the Law." Love is the very spirit and essence of the Law. The Law is to me the highest expression of what I OUGHT to be, in my relations to my Creator and in my relations to my fellow creatures. Now, can what ought to be ever be abrogated? Does it stand to sense? Can the rightness of things ever be altered? Can God ever make two and two five, and can God make evil good and good evil? He can make an evil person good, by saving him from the evil and making him good; but God cannot make evil itself good, and good evil, and He never professes to do it.

Oh, this confounding of things! how it does ruin and befog poor souls! How can it ever be less the duty of the creature to love and serve the Creator than it was when he first came pure and spotless from His hand? How can it ever be less my duty to love my neighbour as myself than it was at the beginning, or how can I satisfy my conscience with less than loving all men with a pure, benevolent love, such as God bears to them in my measure, and according to my capacity? The same standard remains, and the difference between God's scheme of salvation and the scheme of salvation so (almost) universally preached now, is that man's scheme proposes to get me into heaven without fulfilling this Law, while God's scheme proposes to give me power to ·FULFIL IT. Alas! I am afraid many will not find out which is the right one till they get to the Judgment Seat and find it is too late!

Now, I say, that there is not a word, rightly understood and interpreted by correlative Scriptures, in the whole New Testament that disparages or sets aside the Law of God — not a word! Do you think the Apostle was as unphilosophical as many now-a-days? Did he not know what he wrote? Is he not as clear as a bell? And now he comes to the climax of his argument, the great end and purpose towards which he has been advancing in his preceding reasonings:

"THAT the righteousness of the Law might he FULFILLED in us." As though he had said, "This great and glorious end which was lost in Adam shall be re-found and restored." So the old serpent shall be circumvented at last, and God's people shall be able to fulfil this beautiful ideal of rectitude and righteousness which God has planned for man — Jesus Christ shall destroy the work of the devil, restore man, and enable him to walk in the light even as He is in the light. What the Law tried to do by a constraining power from without, the Gospel does by an inspiring power from within. That is the difference. I could not keep it in the letter, but, united to my heavenly Bridegroom, I can keep it in the Spirit. He fills me with His love, and this enables me to keep the Law, for love is the fulfilling of the Law. "Love worketh no'ill to his neighbour" of any kind, and, again, the great Teacher said, "For all the Law is fulfilled in one word —Thou shall love thy neighbour as thyself." If you do that, will you injure your neighbour? See how the spirit fulfills the Law! If you love your neighbour, will you misrepresent him, cheat him, envy him anything that he possesses or enjoys? "No," you say, "of course not; it is a contradiction." Very well, then, get this love in your soul and you will fulfil the Law. Love is the fulfilling of the Law, and he that loveth in this sense dwelleth in God and God in him. Love is the fulfilling of the Law, and the great glory of the Gospel of Christ is that it brings us back to love His Law, and, as the angels delight in it, and, as all holy intelligences delight in it, so we delight in it; and the righteousness of the Law—high, deep, and broad, and long as it is—shall be fulfilled in us, "who walk not after the flesh, but after the Spirit."

Then, I say, the Apostle evidently considered this fulfilment of the Law of Righteousness in us as the highest end of our existence and of redemption: for, he says, it is all to be, that the righteousness of the Law may be fulfilled in us. Mark, not that its claims shall be abated. Oh! not one jot or tittle shall ever be abated. They cannot. God could not abate them. Not that the righteousness of the Law shall cease to have a claim upon you. Oh! if He could have saved us like that, Christ need not have come at all. He could have saved us without a Mediator. No, no! but that the righteousness of the Law may be FULFILLED in us as it was in Him. That we should be brought to the full stature of men and women in Christ Jesus, that we should have this spirit of our heavenly Bridegroom, by which we fulfil the Law, and the servant, in his measure, shall be as his Lord.

How? As I explained, last Sunday, first: We shall be

delivered from the reigning, condemning power of the Law by virtue of an infinite, vicarious sacrifice punished in our stead, and then, married to Him, we shall serve in the newness of the spirit, and not in the oldness of the letter.

I want to be eminently and intensely practical, for the sake of the hungering and thirsting souls who are asking me in their letters, " Tell me how ? Help me ? "

Just let us look at this result (in fourth verse). People talk about glorifying Christ; but, it seems to me, this does glorify Him. It seems to me here is something to glory in, that He has circumvented the old serpent and snatched the prey from his teeth, and restored it, and enabled man, after all, to fulfil the righteousness of God. Not only in what Christ does for us ; but what He does IN US, that God should look on you and say, "I am well pleased. There is nothing there contrary to my will." He will give you the testimony, as He did Enoch, that your ways please Him, that your thoughts please Him, that your motives, and purposes, and desires, and actions please Him. That is what the Gospel proposes to do. We have seen how this spirit is produced. Now let us look at the fruits, and first

This fruit is brought forth in THE AFFECTIONS !

Those people who are thus united to Christ fulfil the Law in their affections. You know it is commonly said, that if you get hold of the affections of a man or a woman you get hold of him or her. So you do. This is the touchstone, and there is nothing in which I have been so grieved and disappointed as in the manifest want of quickness, livingness in the affections of God's people for Him. Oh! how I have seen this come out. The coldness, the unsympathetic character of a great many people's religion, and yet people whom one would not like to unchristianize. I cannot ex-

plain it by any better term than want of quickness. I have
often been struck with the difference when you touch indi-
viduals on some point that affects them personally and on
those which relate to the Kingdom of God, and have been
tempted to say with the Apostle: "All men seek their own,
and not the things that are Jesus Christ's." You talk with
a lady about the salvation of her children's souls, the souls
of her neighbors, and her servants, or about the cause of God
in general, and she will talk "good" with you, so to speak,
and you will feel, yes, it is all very well, but it doesn't seem
to come up from the depths. It seems to come from the
throat, so to speak; a sort of superficial, surface kind of
thing. But, if a child is dangerously ill, how quick the
mother's sympathies, how ready to listen, how willing to do
anything that you suggest to help the child. If the business
is in danger, if a man has got into difficulties and you can
suggest any plan by which he may get out of them, how
quickly his attention is aroused. His interest doesn't flag,
because the subject touches him to the quick. It is his con-
cern, and just so in many other things. God forbid I should
judge all Christians. No, no, no!—there are many blessed
exceptions. There are many like David—rivers of water
do run down their eyes; but I am speaking of the mass of
professors. I am afraid that in their affections there is a
great deal of this lukewarm superficiality. Why is it? Because such people do not abide in Christ, if ever they were
in Him. They do not keep the freshness and the quickness
of the Spirit of Jesus. They do not give themselves time
to do it for one thing, or care about it for another. We want
the constant indwelling of the Holy Spirit to quicken our
spiritual perceptions and keep us awake. It is Satan's great
desire to rock us to sleep, and there is no quality in which

the disciples have been more conspicuous than in going to sleep since the time when the professed watchers went to sleep in the garden; but Jesus, in his mercy and love, is always wakening them. But, oh! this disposition to go to sleep, to lose our quickness of perception. Now, friends, what must you do? You must do as you did at first. Cry and believe till your soul is filled with the love of God.

I shall never forget reading, when only fourteen years of age, a sentiment of a precious and valiant soldier of the Lord Jesus, who is now in glory. Speaking of putting a test, he said that people might easily find out whether they loved God or themselves best: "Suppose you were in business in a little village and were doing pretty well, and everything was going smoothly with you; but there was nothing for you to do there for the Kingdom of God. no particular way in which you could serve or glorify God; and suppose there was another little village hard by, where there was nothing whatever doing for the Kingdom. and you felt it laid upon your soul to go there in order that you might preach to unconverted people and raise a church. and do something for souls. Ah! but you have got a nice business and you don't know whether you would prosper or not in the other village. Now you may know whether you are serving God or yourself first, by this test. If you are seeking God, you will be ready to go to that strange village and trust Him with the consequences; but, if you are serving yourself, you will stop where you are." The Lord has helped me to apply that many a time to many things beside business, and to keep the Kingdom of God FIRST, as I made up my mind it should be first always — not in time merely, but in degree — all the way through. If I love Him best, I shall feel for Him deepest, and shall act for Him first. If I love Him best, I shall feel for Him more deeply than for my husband or children, near and precious as they are, and dearer than my own life a thousand times; but He will be dearer still and His interests; and if, as Jesus Christ says, His interests require me to sacrifice these precious and beloved ones of my soul, then I shall sacrifice them; for the philosophical reason that I love Him better than I love them, and, therefore, I shall lay them on His altar to promote His glory. If I understand it, this is the fruit of the Spirit in the affections — God first. I am afraid, in a great many instances, it is husband first, wife first, children first, and, I am afraid, in some cases, business first, and then God may take what there is left, and be thankful for that! Now, anybody in this condition need not expect joy, peace, power. You will never get it, if you do. God will have to make you over again before you can get it, and to alter the conditions of His salvation. Oh! but if you will lay it all down, that is quite another thing.

As I said to a lady, a little time ago, "The Lord can take your husband, if you refuse to give him to Him;" and I am afraid God's people often compel Him to take their darlings, because they make them idols; whereas, if they had laid them on His altar, they might have them back, as Abraham received back Isaac. I said to a gentleman, "Mind, God does not burn down your barns, wreck your ships, and take away your riches. God loves your soul enough to do it, if you let these things prevent that whole-hearted consecration which He requires." We are in His hands. "Whom He loveth He chasteneth," and if you want to keep the precious things you have, oh! put them at His feet, and hold them in subordination to Him. First, in your affections! He is a jealous God, and jealousy in God is very much like jealousy in us. It is the same characteristic of mind, only purified from selfishness.   He is a jealous God, and if you will love these things better than Him, and if you will not give Him your affections, then He will chstise you, or, what is worse still, He will take His Holy Spirit from you.

Fruit in your affections.   Oh, if Christ had your affections, how it would operate in everything!   The wife would not be always grumbling because the husband had to go out three or four evenings a week on the Lord's errands—only let them be the Lord's errands.   The husband would not grudge to give his wife up to go to help to win souls, because it deprived him of her society or a few comforts that she might provide for him if she were near.   The parents would not grudge to restrain their children as Eli did.   He did not restrain them from that which they liked, and you know the fruit it brought.   Parents who love God best will not allow their children to learn anything which could not be pressed into the service of God.   They do not allow them to run with the giddy multitude, to dance or do anything the devil might inspire them to desire.   "No!" they will say, "my children belong to God, and I am going to train them for God and God only."   Bless the Lord, He helped me to make up my mind to do that before I became a mother; and he has helped me to keep that promise (though I have not been as faithful to it as I ought), casting aside resolutely every temptation to the contrary.   And now He is giving me the fruit of my self-denial in the souls and labors of my precious children. One after another, as they grow up, they take their natural place in the temple of the Lord, and I believe they shall go out no more forever.   Oh, that parents would do it! Parents might save their children.   I know what a mother's feelings are.   I know the temptation there is to see them shine in competition with others, and to excel others.   I know it all; but I said, "No; 'Get thee behind me, Satan.'" I will keep them for God; and He has enabled me to keep them for Him. Bless His holy name!

I loved Him better than I loved them, and, much as I loved them (and those who know me know I do love them), I would see them in a row laid in their coffins before I would sacrifice His interests and lose their souls. Do you love Him best?· Test yourself. Do you love Him more than all else? Are you holding everything in subordination to Him?

Further, this fruit will come out in our members — our bodies; and oh, there is a deep spiritual meaning which, I trust, many of you know, in those words of the Apostle, "For the body is dead because of sin; but He hath quickened even your mortal bodies by His Spirit, which dwelleth in you." It is killed to the Devil, as well as to sin, and all the uses of Satan; but it is quickened by the Spirit for the use of God so that you can render not only the calves of your lips, but your hands, and eyes, and brain, and heart, and feet, and the whole of your body to Him — your members instruments of righteousness unto God. Hence, such a person will not feel their eyes are their own, to rove at random wherever they list. Such a person will not feel his tongue is his own, to speak as he pleases. He will "bridle it," as James says, when tempted to speak unadvisedly. Such a person will not feel that his hands are his own, to waste the time, in which he ought to be doing something for God. Such a person will not feel that his feet are his own, to carry him where he lists, but where his Master would have him go — his whole body consecrated, and, especially his tongue — consecrated to God, to testify for Him. He will feel that he must feed his body, as my husband often says, on the same principle that a man feeds his horse — to keep it in the best working condition for

God — never eating anything that will bring the devils of dyspepsia dancing round his soul. And, not only so with eating and drinking, but all his surroundings and deportment must be in keeping. It is the Lord's body; and if you love Him best, you will keep it for Him.

This fruit will also appear in our family relations. We shall fulfil the Law to our neighbours. You see, God wants only what we have. He is not a hard master, and the Great Teacher said, "This is the law and the prophets." This is the great commandment, embracing all the rest, "Thou shalt love the Lord thy God with all thy heart, and mind, and soul, and strength," and the second is like unto it, "And thy neighbor as thyself;" and the man who does that is a perfect man, fulfils the law; and when you have the fulness of love that enables you to love God best and your neighbor as yourself — enables you to do for the souls and bodies of your fellows what you would that they should do for you, if they had your light and were in your circumstances, then the law is fulfilled in you. Such people cannot sit 365 days in the year at the table with unconverted people and never try to get them saved. Such people cannot abide in the same house with unbelievers and not make them miserable. Oh, no. The unconverted say, "It's too wretched to live here. I must get out of this crying and praying for me all day long." As a servant once said, she couldn't stand it. She had had praying enough at home, without coming there to have it. She did stand it for six weeks, and broke down at family altar, GOT SAVED, and became a preacher afterward. This spirit of love will make every unconverted sinner within your reach so miserable that they will have to be converted or run away. How would you do if he were DYING? You would run about in every direction to get a minister. What a pity you did not feel like this twelve years ago. You might have got the sinner converted then, and he have been serving the Lord all this time? But, now he is dying, what a stir you make. What a purely selfish religion that is. You want him saved, so that he may get into HEAVEN, not that he might serve, honour, and glorify God. You don't care at all about that. He might live on in disobedience. Oh, be as much concerned for the honour of God as you are for your friends' salvation at the last, and then God will know how to save them.

This fruit will also appear in your church relations. It will bring forth fruit. As the Apostle says, "Exhorting one another daily, not suffering sin in your neighbour; reproving each other, and confessing you faults the one to the other." Where is any of it done? I should like very much to attend such a meeting, if you invite me, where Christians really and honestly confess their faults one to the other and pray for one another, beseeching the Lord to heal them in those particular points where they have failed, telling one another of the deep things of God, and talking lovingly and freely to one another as they used to do. The communion of saints — exhorting one another daily. The devil is at it daily. The world is plying for us daily. The flesh is there daily. Everything else goes on daily. Why should not this exhorting one another, confessing your faults to one another, and praying for one another, go on daily, too?

Is it a fact that we are each other's keeper? Is it a fact that God will require for our influence over other souls? I believe it is.

Then in our relations to the world ——. But I forestalled this in my address on "Aggressive Effort." And now let us go down on our knees before God and ask Him to work this love in us, and give us this spirit, that we may thus FULFIL THIS LAW in all its relations.

WITNESSING FOR CHRIST.

"Ye shall be witnesses unto me both in Jerusalem, and in all Judea, and in Samaria, and unto the uttermost parts of the earth." — ACTS i. 8.
"And ye are witnesses of these things." — ACTS v. 32.

Again and again the same vocation and commission is bestowed upon the apostles and disciples. To the ends of the earth and to the end of time this commission comes down to everyone of the Lord's own, for He says: "Go ye into all the world and preach the Gospel to every creature, and, lo, I will be with you always, even unto the end of the world." That embraces us. And to every disciple who has preceded, or is to follow us, is promised His Divine Presence in this glorious work of testifying for Him.

God needs witnesses in this world.

Why? Because the whole world is in revolt against Him. The world has gone away from God. The world ignores God, denies, contradicts His testimony, misunderstands His character, government, and purposes, and is gone off into utter and universal revolt and rebellion. Now if God is to keep any hold upon man at all, and have any influence with him, He must be represented down here. There was no other way of doing it. If you get a province of this realm in anarchy and rebellion, unless there be a party in the province to represent the Queen and the govern-

ment, it will go altogether and be lost to the kingdom for
ever; there must be a party to represent the rightful
sovereign, the law and the government. So God must be
represented, and, praise His name, He has had His faithful
witnesses from the beginning until now. As the Apostle
says — "He left not Himself without witnesses." Down
from the days of Enoch, who walked with God, to this
present hour, God has always had His true and faithful
witnesses. In the worst times there have been some burning and shining lights. Sometimes few and far between,
sometimes, like Noah, one solitary man in a whole generation of men, witnessing for God — but there *has been one.*
God has not left Himself without witnesses.

But Jesus Christ the Son, the well-beloved of the Father
— He was *the great Witness.* He came especially to manifest, to testify of, and to reveal the Father to men. This
was His great work. He came not to testify of Himself
but of His Father, not to speak His own words, but the
words His Father gave Him to speak. He came to reveal
God to men. He was *the* great Witness. And when He
had to leave the world and go back to His Father, then He
commissioned His disciples to take His place and to be God's
witnesses on earth. And oh! friends, God's *real people* are
His *only* witnesses. He will not allow angels — we do not
know why — to witness for Him here. He has called man
to witness for Him, — His people — "Ye are my witnesses."

Jesus gave a good testimony — did He not? He witnessed nobly, constantly, bravely of His Father, and sealed
His testimony with His blood. The world treated Him as
it has treated most of God's faithful witnesses from the
beginning; it persecuted Him; it slew Him, as it *would*
every faithful witness for God — if God allowed it — and

would leave itself without a single spiritual light: for the spirit that worketh in the children of disobedience hath an eternal and devilish hatred of every real, living, spiritual child of God. It hates Him as it hated the Son Himself, and it is not the devil's fault if he does not extinguish and exterminate every such witness. It is because God will not allow him, but holds us, keeps us, saves us, in spite of him.

The Lord commissioned, then, His disciples to be His witnesses, and He said — oh! beautiful words, and yet, how much they involve which few understand — "As Thou hast sent Me into the world, even so send I them into the world." *Even so :* as Thou hast sent Me to be Thy representative in the world, to spend and be spent for Thee, and shed My blood for Thee, if necessary, so send I them; — and so He did send them, and they had just the same fare as their Master, and many of them just the same end. But they were faithful witnesses, and they went forward and testified everywhere, to the Jews and to the Gentiles, in the Temple and in the market-place, by the wayside and in the highways and hedges — they went and testified of this Saviour, and charged the wicked Jews with His crucifixion, and God accompanied their testimony by the Spirit, and thousands upon thousands were converted — turned from their rebellion to God.

Now, the fact that witnessing is necessary shows that *there is controversy going on in the world* as to the things and claims of God — that there are two sides to this, as to every other case. The great mass of mankind say that God's truth is a lie. They say it virtually, if they do not say it in words, and many thousands of them, alas! in words, also. They deny, many of them, His very existence, and say there is neither Heaven nor Hell — that Jesus Christ was a mere man — that religion is a myth, and that there is no such thing as the knowledge of forgiveness of sins — that this witnessing is a grand delusion, and that there is nothing of the kind!

Now, Christ calls His people to go and be witnesses to these facts. Witnesses, you know, must deal with facts, not theories — not what they think and believe, merely, but what they *know*. Now, God wants His people to witness to facts — to something that has been done, and is being done — something that is, and continues to be — fact.

And He wants us to be GOOD witnesses, too. Oh! how much depends upon the character of a witness even in an earthly court. If you can cast a reflection upon the previous character or veracity of a witness, you shake his testimony, and take away its value. Oh! how important that Christ's witnesses should be good witnesses — that is, that they should fairly and truly represent Him and His truth — for, if they misrepresent Him, somebody is sure to be damned through their inconsistency — and, oh! to have the blood of souls upon our skirts! To misrepresent a man, or woman, or child, is bad enough, but to misrepresent God! — to show a caricature of the religion of Jesus Christ! — to say to people, virtually, "Look at me: this is the religion of Jesus Christ — the way I live and act — WHAT I AM." I say, such a man had far better have had a millstone hanged about his neck and been drowned in the depths of the sea. There would, then, be an end of his mischief; but a false witness for Jesus Christ is the greatest traitor on the face of the earth. He does more harm than a thousand false earthly witnesses. Oh! my friends, to be *good* witnesses for Jesus Christ! The more a witness is supposed to know of the truth to which he testifies, the greater his responsibility. Oh!

for a minister to be a bad witness, as some of the prophets of old were. Look at the awful things God says about them that lead His people into the ditch, caring more about the fleece than the sheep—awful! For a mother to be a bad witness in her family, and to take her little children, clinging on to her skirts, right to the edge of the pit! For a master to be a bad witness—to profess to be a Christian and to be a bad witness before his men; for a Sunday-school teacher to be a bad, inconsistent, false witness of Jesus Christ in his class; for members of Christian churches to be bad witnesses to one another, and to the world; who can tell the awful results? Oh! it is this inconsistent witnessing that has lowered and lowered the standard of practical Christianity till we have not got any standard left—till the landmarks are so obliterated that there are not any to be seen.

FAITHFUL witnesses! He wants us to be faithful witnesses.

I want to note *one or two qualifications of a faithful witness*, and, oh, may the Holy Spirit help us.

The first qualification, then, of a faithful witness, is, *A personal knowledge of the facts to which he witnesses.* If a witness in a court of justice begins to talk of what he thinks, feels, and believes—"oh! hush, hush," says the judge, "we can't have that; we want to know what you KNOW—what you have seen, heard, and felt of this case;" and these are the sort of witnesses Jesus Christ wants, who can get up and say "I KNOW!" The sort of witness that St. Paul was, who could look his judge in the face and say, "I would that thou wert altogether such as I am, save these bonds." What an impudent man he must have been, if he was not a sanctified man. What a supreme egotist! Those

are the sort of witnesses. How Agrippa must have felt,
just then. How the tables were turned. "Oh! I am turned
into the dock, and here is the prisoner taking his seat upon
the bench." That is the sort of witnessing we want. "I
would that thou wert *altogether* such as I am, except these
chains." Could you stand up in the dock and say that?
Could you stand up in your own house and say it? Could
you stand up *anywhere* and say it? That is what the Lord
Jesus Christ wants — people who know, who experience, who
realize, who live the things they witness to. This is what
the world is dying for — people who can get up and say, "I
KNOW." The Lord wants people to tell the world they
are saved. Can you? They will begin to listen to you,
then. You will begin to have some effect upon them. They
will begin to open their eyes and ears, and wonder whether
it will be possible for God to save them. That is altogther
different to a fine-spun theory *about* religion — telling them
that God has SAVED YOU. Not what we have learned in
books. The world is sick of that. I don't wonder at intelligent men flying off from religion. I can make great excuse
when I think what many of them have to listen to from
Sunday to Sunday. As a gentleman said to me, "It's
enough to sicken anybody. We do get something in the
papers, but, upon my word, I can't keep awake at church.
It is not that I would not, if I could, but I can't." Poor
fellow! — how I pitied him.

No! not what is got from books; not a dry, fine-spun
theory, from mere hearsay. When a witness begins with
what he heard someone say, "oh, hush!" says the judge,
"we don't want that, we want to know what you have seen.
Keep to the facts." Jesus Christ wants you to keep to the
facts. Tell them, as John says, what you have seen, and

heard, and handled, and realized of the truth of God. *Personal knowledge!* It is wonderful how simple salvation language is, when you have learnt it by experience, and are prepared to speak plainly to the people.

Then, a faithful witness must *tell the truth, and the whole truth.* He must not hold back anything on account of personal inconvenience, suffering, loss, or gain — the whole truth. Oh! I tremble to think what will be the fate of some who set themselves up as teachers, and who have kept back part of the truth because, to their apprehension, it was not palatable or profitable to mankind. What have I got to do with that? I have to preach the truth — the beautiful, whole, round, diamond, luminous with Divine light, and not split down the middle and made into damning error, by which Satan is carrying down thousands to Hell. The whole truth — both sides: the side that relates to God, and the side that relates to man, and be done with the nonsense of making God contradict Himself, for "God is light, and in Him is no darkness at all." If there were contradictions, there would be darkness. No; the darkness is in our own poor, little, puny brains, and not in God or in His Book. In His Book, rightly interpreted, there is no contradiction whatsoever. The *whole* truth: the convicting truth as well as the healing truth; the sword as well as the balm; the running in of the Divine knife as well as the pouring in of the Divine oil. As Paul says, in the 26th chapter and 18th verse, "To open their eyes, and to turn them from darkness to light, and from the power of Satan unto God, that they may receive forgiveness of sins." He says he preached to the Jews and Gentiles that they should repent. This is the Apostle Paul, the great expounder of Justification by Faith, "That they should repent," and what?

— oh, you legal Paul, what?— "Do works meet for repentance." Oh, Paul, I thought you were saved from works altogether, and had done with the Law. Oh! you preach works, and doing works meet for repentance. That is not Gospel, Paul! He significantly adds, "For this cause the Jews caught me, and tried to kill me :" and for that cause the Pharisees have been trying to kill God's true, whole-truth witnesses ever since, for they don't like the doctrine that cuts idols and sin in twain, and that says, "Bring forth fruits meet for repentance."

The faithful witness must give the whole truth; and he must give it personally, too. A faithful witness must give it himself. He can't witness by proxy. He may pay one hundred and fifty witnesses to go and witness for him : that is all right. It is no more than he ought to do — two hundred and fifty, if he has money enough — because the Master claims all that he has, little or much, every farthing of it.

Therefore he can never do any more than he ought, when he has done all; but that will not exonerate him from the obligation. If I have put my candle in you, it is that it may shine for somebody else's benefit. If I have given you the bread of life, it is for you to go and break it to the famishing multitudes round about you. YE are my witnesses. You may pay the ministers and the missionary, but you must do it yourself, too, for how can *one* witness make up *for two?* True, God wants the minister to witness, and it is no more than his duty if he witnesses all day long as long as he lives. But that will never make up for your lack of service. YOU must witness; and *there are some souls with whom you have more influence than any other living being,* — some souls that you can better get at than any other person — some souls that, if you do not save, will, probably,

never be saved at all. Ye are my witnesses, and, if ye have
the grace and love and light of God, it is at the peril of
your soul if you hide it.

Then, in the next place, *faithful witnesses must speak out,
not mince the matter*—not "mumble," as they say in court.
The judge makes the witness speak up so that everybody
may hear him. *He must be heard.* "Speak out." And why
should not the Lord's witnesses speak out ? I wonder when
we shall be done with this sneaking, hole and corner, shame-
faced religion! I wonder when Christian England will
cease to be ashamed of its God!! The only nation under
Heaven ashamed of its religion and its God is the one that
has got the true God to worship and to love. What an anomaly! Speak out!!

David knew nothing about this mincing, half-and-half,
milk-and-water sort of religion. David rejoiced to tell of
His righteousness before the great congregation. He was
always telling about His goodness, and His law, and singing
about it all the day long, dancing before the ark sometimes,
and doing all manner of demonstrative things to glorify his
God. And that was not enough, for when he had called
upon all human kind to praise Him, he called on the hills
and the trees to clap their hands and to dance for joy. We
want some of *that* sort of religion now-a-days. Talk of the
new dispensation, I wish we could get a bit of that back.

The interests of truth demand this outspokenness. How
is error to be met but by the bold proclamation of the truth ?
How are the emissaries of Satan palming upon mankind his
lies — always at it, night and day — how are they to be
silenced but by witnesses faithfully crying in their ears,
"This is a lie, and that is a lie. This is the truth and this
is the way; we know, we see, we feel — walk ye in it."

Turn ye, turn ye, for why will ye die ? They want out-spoken witnesses. There are plenty of false witnesses now as there ever were, and what does Jesus Christ want ? He wants His true witnesses to come out and face them, and be a match for them,— not to sneak away in holes and corners, and be ashamed of it and talk about an unobtrusive religion —unobtrusive nonsense! There is no such thing! Come out before the world. If He be God, speak for Him. As Elijah said, "If He be God serve Him, but if Baal, serve HIM." Then away with all this nonsense, your sanctuaries, and Bibles, and profession — have done with it all and follow Baal. Be one thing or the other. If he be God serve him. And methinks there wants an Elijah now to come and ring it all through England. I would like to see any man get up and make a straightforward recognition of and appeal to, God, in our Houses of Parliament, and I would like to see how he would be greeted.

I was thinking, as I was passing the Royal Exchange, and saw on the top " The earth is the Lord's and the fullness thereof," how many believed it who walked beneath its shadow. I wonder what anyone would be thought of were he practically to recognise the fact. " Oh ! " they would say, "he's not fit for his post — you'll have to take him away; he's a little affected in his head." Oh! you know it is so ; but God is not mocked, though men think He is. God sits in the circle of Heaven, and though the people do rage, and the heathen imagine a vain thing, and the kings of the earth set themselves, He is laughing at them, and by-and-by will come their calamity.

We say the world is dying ; — what for ? Sermons ? No. Periodicals ? No. Religious stories ? Oh ! dear, no. There is no chance of a want of them for many a long year to come.

Dying for disquisitions ? No. For fine-spun theories ? No. For creeds and faiths ? Oh! you might have them by the dozen. What is it dying for ? — downright, straightforward, honest, loving, earnest testimony about what God can do FOR SOULS. *That* is what it wants. That is what those poor men in the shops, those walking up and down Oxford Street, in the theatres, in the dancing saloons, in the concert rooms — everywhere, that is what men want: somebody to come and take them lovingly by the collar, and tell them that God is God, and that He can save them. "He has saved me, my brother, and He can save you!" *That* is what the world wants. One word like that is better than a sermon, and it will do more for God and the salvation of the world. Oh, yes, men are saying, in fact all over this land — thousands, "Here I am; I am a poor slave of sin. I know it." They say it in their consciences though they do not say it to you. They say it often to us when they are pushed into a corner by the sword of the Spirit. "I know I am wrong, sinful, wicked." As that dear John Allen, whose life I have been telling about, said once when sitting swearing, surrounded by his companions, and somebody said to him, "Jock, if you were to die, what would become of you ? " "I should go to hell, straight!" He was an honest fellow. He knew where he was going, and he said it.

I said to a gentleman, "Mr. So-and-so, what about your soul ? " He said, "It's in a devilish state." Poor man! He knew where he was going, and there are thousands like him. Do you think they don't feel their bondage ? Have they not got a mind and a conscience ? Have they not a better side, as you call it, to their nature ? Has not God flashed the light of His Holy Spirit upon their dark souls, and have they not struggled and striven ? Yes, but they say,

"There is no health in us; there is no help for us. We have done making resolutions and trying to be better; we cannot. There is no hope in us." And there they are, waiting for somebody to come and tell them there is HELP IN GOD. They say, "I see precious little difference in you religious folks; I have never known anybody that religion has seemed to do much for." And, when they are told to believe, they laugh at you, and I don't wonder at it. The poor human conscience is better instructed than many of its teachers. It wants to be put RIGHT, and it says, is there any hope? Can God save such as I am? Has He saved anybody like me from this thraldom, from this slavery, from this misery, from this constantly going down in the mud? Did he ever *save* anybody LIKE ME? And sometimes he goes to chapel or church, and hopes the minister will tell him, when lo, he begins a dissertation about the resurrection, or the divinity of Christ, or something the man has believed all his life, and so he is disappointed again, and he says, "This is of no use to me." Oh! friends, I speak the things I know from the testimony of scores of souls. In fact, I could not repeat it, it would make your faces burn to hear what men of intelligence, thought and standing, have said to me in many an ante-room where I have been labouring. It is time there was a change. The world is famishing for lack of real spiritual bread. It wants something to eat, and you give it a stone! but *God is raising a people who know what it wants and how to give it*, who know how to break the bread of life, and testify what God has done for them, and what he can do for other poor famishing souls; who can say: "Here, my friend, He can save such as you. I was such an one once. I was a slave of sin, the slave of drink, or a blasphemer, or a liar, or a thief, or addicted to some bad secret habit worse than any of these. I was such a slave, and he has saved me. He has broken my fetters and set me free, and I am the Lord's free-man. He has saved me and He can save you." That is what the world wants — TESTIMONY WITNESSING.

Has He saved any of you? Are you testifying to your poor, famishing, sinking fellow-men? Do you ever look at them and think where they are going? Do you pity them, love them, long after them in the bowels of Jesus Christ? Do you know anything of that longing? If so, how can you forbear testifying? " Ye are my witnesses of these things," everywhere, at all times, amongst all people!!

It is in the nature of the case that a *witness must witness before other people*, before living hearers. That is the place to witness, and before enemies, and when he does not know which way the wind will blow, or how the words of God will be received. He must be a true witness, even if he has to seal his testimony with his blood.

This was the kind of witnessing the martyrs did. I often wonder whether there would be any martyrs now. Sometimes I think that the greatest boon to the Church of Christ would be a time of persecution. I believe it would. I believe it would drive us up to God and each other. We should find out, then, whether we were willing to forsake all to follow Him. You know that if the martyrs had taken the standard of religious life that exists now, they would never have been martyrs. They would have looked after their own skins, and left the Lord to look after the Gospel. If they might have been allowed a little latitude, and gone half way, there would not have been any martyrs, because they could nearly all have got off with that; but they felt it necessary to be faithful right through, and to stand by the truth to the very last jot and tittle, and when they could have got off by saying three words on a paper, they refused to do it, and went to the stake, and let the flames lick up their blood. Those are the witnesses the Lord wants — outside, everywhere, always at it. Always witnessing. "Always?" you say. Yes; always. Why? *Because men are always dying and being damned!* —if the Bible is true—everywhere — your friends and your neighbors around you. You get a letter: "Oh! Mr. So-and-so is dead — only ill three days — thirty-six hours — twenty-four hours — gone!" Ah! and the echo in many a soul afterwards is, "What would I give to go and have one talk with him." But he's gone — *somewhere!* Where is he gone? If he were unwashed and unpardoned and unsaved — where is he gone? I got so wrought up once upon this point that I thought I should have lost my reason. I could not sleep at night with thinking of the state of those who die unsaved. Dare I think about it? WHERE IS HE GONE?

Oh! it was this view of the case that led me to open my mouth first in public for God.

I have promised some friends here to-night to give this illustration from my own experience, or else I rarely refer to it. I had long had a controversy on this question in my soul. In fact, from the time I was converted, the Spirit of God had constantly been urging me into paths of usefulness and labour, which seemed to me impossible. Perhaps some of you would hardly credit that I was one of the most timid and bashful disciples the Lord Jesus ever saved· For ten years of my Christian life my life was one daily battle with the cross — not because I wilfully rejected, as many do, for that I never dared to do. Oh, no! I used to make up my mind I would, and resolve and intend, and then, when the hour came, I used to fail for want of courage. I need not have failed. I now see how foolish I was, and how wrong; but, for some four or five months before I commenced speaking, the controversy had been signally roused in my soul which God had awakened years before, but which, through mistaken notions, fear, and timidity, I had almost allowed to die out. I was brought to very severe heart-searchings at this time. I had not been realizing so much of the Divine presence. I had lost a great deal of the power and happiness I once enjoyed. During a season of sickness, one day it seemed as if the Lord revealed it all to me by His Spirit. I had no vision, but a revelation to my mind. He seemed to take me back to the time when I was fifteen and sixteen, when I first gave my heart to Him. He seemed to show me all the bitter way, how this one thing had been the fly in the pot of ointment, the bitter in the cup, and prevented me from realizing what I should otherwise have done. I felt how it had hindered the revelation of Himself to me, and hindered me from growing in grace, and learning more of the deep things of God. He showed it to me, and then I remember prostrating myself upon my face before Him, and I promised Him there in the sick-room : "Lord, if Thou wilt return unto me, as in the days of old, and re-visit me with those urgings of Thy Spirit which I used to have, I will obey, if I die in the attempt. I care not ; I will obey." However, the Lord did not re-visit me immediately. He let me recover, and I went out again. About three months after that I went to the chapel of which my husband was a minister, and he had an extraordinary service. Even then he was trying something new to get the outside people. They were having a meeting in which ministers and friends in the town were taking part, and all giving their testimony and speaking for God. I was in the minister's pew, with my eldest boy, then four years old, and there were some thousand people present. I felt much more depressed than usual in spirit, and not expecting anything particular, but, as the testimonies went on, I felt the Spirit come upon me. You alone who have felt it know what it means. It cannot be described. I felt it to the extremities of my fingers and toes. It seemed as if a voice said to me, "Now, if you were to go and testify, you know I would bless it to your own soul as well as to the souls of the people," and I gasped again, and I said in my soul, "Yes, Lord, I believe Thou wouldst, but I cannot do it." I had forgotten my vow— it did not occur to me at all. All in a moment, after I had said that to the Lord, I seemed to see the bedroom where I had lain, and to see myself as though I had been there prostrate before the Lord promising Him that, and then the voice seemed to say to me, "Is this consistent with that promise?" and I almost jumped up and said, "No, Lord, it is the old thing over again, but I cannot do it," and I felt as though I would sooner die than do it. And then the Devil said, "Besides, you are not prepared to speak. You will look like a fool, and have nothing to say." He made a mistake. He overdid himself for once. It was that word settled it. I said, "Ah! this is just the point. I have never yet been willing to be a fool for Christ, now I will be one ; " and without stopping another moment, I rose up in the seat, and walked up the chapel. My dear husband was just going to conclude. He thought something had happened to me, and so did the people. We had been there two years, and they knew my timid, bashful nature. He stepped down to ask me, "What is the matter, my dear?" I said, "I want to say a word."

He was so taken by surprise, he could only say, "My dear wife wants to say a word," and sat down. He had been trying to persuade me to do it for ten years. He and a lady in the church, only that very week, had been trying to persuade me to go and address a little cottage meeting, of some twenty working people, but could not. I got up — God only knows how — and if any mortal ever did hang on the arm of Omnipotence, I did. I felt as if I were clinging to some human arm — and yet it was a Divine arm — to hold me. I just got up and told the people how it came about. I confessed, as, I think, everybody should, when they have been in the wrong and misrepresented the religion of Jesus Christ. I told the people, although I had been occupying all the ordinary positions of a minister's wife, though I was young then I had been doing a great deal more than many an elderly one does in the church of God, in the way of meeting believers, and visiting and working behind the scenes, so that they had all been regarding me as a very devoted woman, and I told them so. I said, "I dare say many of you have been regarding me as a very devoted woman, and one who has been living faithfully to God, but I have come to know that I have been living in disobedience, and to that extent I have brought darkness and leanness into my soul, but I promised the Lord three or four months ago, and I dare not disobey. I have come to tell you this, and to promise the Lord that I will be obedient to the Heavenly vision."

But oh! how little I saw then what it involved. I never imagined the life of publicity it was going to lead me into, and of trial also; for I was never allowed to have another quiet Sabbath, when I could speak or stand up. All I took there was the present step. I did not see in advance, but

the Lord, as He always does, when His people are honest
with Him, and obedient, opened the windows of Heaven,
and poured out such a blessing, that there was not room to
contain it.

There was more weeping, they said, in the chapel that
day than ever there had been before. Many dated a renew-
al in righteousness from that very moment, and began a life
of devotion and consecration to God.

Now, I might have "talked good" to them till now, and
that would never have happened. That honest confession,
coming out and testifying the truth, did what twenty years'
talk would never have done.

The work went on. Whenever I spoke, the chapel used
to be crowded to its utmost capacity, and numbers were converted. Not to me, but to God be all the glory. Shame to
me that I did not begin sooner. It was not I that did this,
but the Holy Ghost, the Holy Spirit of God.

The Lord dealt with me in a very wonderful way. Three
months after this, my dear husband fell sick the first time,
and he was obliged to go away into the country. A depu-
tation waited on me, to ask me to take his town appoint-
ments. I said I could not think of such a thing. What
could I do with that great congregation? They must not
ask me — and away they went. They came back again to
know if I would take the nights, they implored and im-
portuned me until I promised. So you see, God forced me
to begin to think and work. I was obliged, and I did it
with four little children, the eldest then four years and
three months old. It looked an inopportune time, did it
not, to begin to preach? It looked as though the Lord
must have made a mistake. However, He gave me grace
and strength, and enabled me to do it; and while I was

nursing my baby, many a time I was thinking of what I was going to say next Sunday, and between times noted down with a pencil the thoughts as they struck me. And then I would appear sometimes, with an outline scratched in pencil, trusting in the Lord to give me the power of His Holy Spirit; and I think I can say that from that day — and it is about nineteen years and nine months since — He has never allowed me to open my mouth without giving me signs of His presence and blessing. Don't you see that while the devil kept me silent, he kept me comparatively fruitless; now I have ground to hope and expect to meet hundreds in glory, whom God has made me instrumental in saving. The Lord dealt very tenderly with me: giving me great encouragement, but some things were dreadful to me at first. I would not go into pulpits till the people demanded it. And the first time I saw my name on a wall! — I shall never forget the sensation. Then my dear husband said, "When you gave yourself to the Lord, did you not give Him your name?" Thus he used to go from one thing to another, until now I have learned to glory in the Cross. When a dear friend was talking, the other day, about the tremendous undertaking it was to go to France and begin there, I said, "My dear sir, I should not feel any more discomposed to go to France, and open there next Sunday, than I should to appear in St. Andrew's Hall, simply for this reason, that I believe God is the same in every place, and the same faith, and the same truths and the same faithfulness will bring Him to our help." "Ye are my witnesses," saith the Lord, " And, lo, I am with you ALWAYS!"

Will you be encouraged, my sister? Never mind trembling. I trembled. Never mind your heart beating. Mine

beat nearly through. Never mind how weak you are. I
have gone many a time from the bed to the pulpit, and back
from the pulpit to bed. It is not by human power, wisdom,
might, or strength — it is by My Spirit, saith the Lord. He
loves to use the weak things, that the excellency may be
seen to be of God. Were your neighbors sick of some devas-
tating plague, and you could go and help them, would not
you do it? Would you say, "I am only a woman, and I cannot?" "Oh," you would say, "let me go, like Miss Night-
ingale did to the sick and wounded soldiers. Let me go."
And these are not the bodies, but the *souls*. They are dying.
They are going to an eternal death. Will you not rise up?
Oh! suppose all the Christians in this hall to-night were to
begin, from this hour, to be faithful, and consistently testifying everywhere for Jesus, what a commotion there would
be! How many, think you, would be converted in a month's
time? How would they begin flocking like doves to the
windows? How would the ministers, some of them, begin
to wake up? The people would go and beseech them morning, noon, and night. God wants you to witness right out
everywhere, in the darkest courts and alleys and in Oxford
Street alike. Begin, and the Spirit of God will fall upon
you, and however they may try to get rid of the Holy Ghost,
they will not be able to do it when God has got hold of them.
We catch thousands of people in this way who never intended to be converted. Every day I live the more I am convinced that if God's people were to be in desperate earnest,
thousands would be won; but they are not likely to be won
by the genteel fashion of putting the truth before them —
so common now-a-days — because nobody thinks they are in
danger! If you believe it, *begin*. The Apostle says you are
to be good, valiant soldiers of Jesus Christ; the old Chris-

tians were all this; they fought a good warfare, and they overcame the devil by the "blood of the Lamb and the *word of their testimony."* Be soldiers for the Lord, and He will give the victory, and you shall go and take prisoners. Great big giants, black-hearted infidels, black-hearted blasphemers, they shall go down before you like little children, because the Lord of Hosts will put His Spirit in you. "Ye are My witnesses!" WITNESS of Me everywhere and always. The Lord help you. Amen.

FILLED WITH THE SPIRIT.

"And being assembled together with them, commanded them that they should not depart from Jerusalem, but wait for the promise of the Father."— ACTS i. 4.

"Be filled with the Spirit."—EPHESIANS v. 18.

I thought, perhaps, it would meet a difficulty of some who are present this afternoon, to state, with respect to last Sabbath's address, that this exhortation, to be filled with the Spirit, is given broadly to all believers. If my remarks, at that time, conveyed the idea to anyone, that there were merely a privileged few who were called to be thus filled with the Spirit — to be, as it were, the leaders of the rest, and others were to abide, and must abide, on a lower platform of Christian experience, I certainly did not intend them to do so. God forbid that I should insinuate anything of the kind, because I do not believe it. I believe that this injunction is given broadly to all believers everywhere, and in all times, and it is as much the privilege of the youngest and weakest believer here to be filled with the Spirit, as it is of the most advanced, if the believer will comply with the conditions, and conform to the injunctions of the Saviour, on which He has promised this gift. I do not find two standards of Christian experience here at all. I do not believe God ever intended there should be a lower life and a higher life, and I am afraid that those people who rest in the lower life will find themselves awfully mistaken at last. I believe that religion is all or nothing. God is either first or He is nowhere with us, individually. The very essence and core of religion is, " God first," and allegiance and obedience to Him first.

If I cannot keep my father and mother and be faithful to God, then I must forsake my father and mother. If I cannot keep my husband or wife, and be faithful to Him, then I must forsake husband or wife. If I cannot keep my children and be faithful to Him, then Jesus Christ says, forsake them. And if I cannot keep my houses and lands and be faithful to Him, then I must forsake them. If I cannot keep my business and be faithful to Him, then I must sacrifice my business, and if I cannot keep my health and be faithful to Him, then I must sacrifice it, and, last of all, if I cannot keep my life and be faithful to Him, then I must be prepared to lose it, and lay my neck on the block, if need be. This is my religion, and I do not know any other. I do not believe any other will stand on the right hand of the throne ; and, if that be so, why, all other sorts must stand on the left. If this be not true, I am utterly and thoroughly mistaken in the first principles of Christianity, and I will come and sit down at anybody's feet who can convince me that I am wrong. So, pray, do not attach that idea to me that I think that any person can sit down, providing he has light, or with opportunities of getting light, without embracing this higher-life religion, and then get into Heaven in this shame-faced, sneaking way. No, no!—God will have you or He will not have you. He will know you or will say, "Depart from me, I know you not." The Lord help you every one.

This Pentecost is offered to all believers. It comes, or it would come, in the experience of every believer, if he would have it. God wants you to have it. God calls you to it. Jesus Christ has bought it for you, and you may have it and live in its power as much as these apostles did, if you will — every one of you. My dear friends, you may have it, be filled with it, and no one but God knows what He would do with you and what he would make of you if you were thus filled, for the experience of Peter shows you how utterly different a man is *before* he gets a Pentecostal baptism and *after* he gets it. The man who could not stand the questionings of a servant-maid before he got this power, dared to be crucified after he got it. I may just say, that here is the great cause of the decline of so many who begin well. "Ye did run well," we might truly say of thousands in this land to-day, "Ye did run well." They begin in the Spirit, and then, as the Apostle says, "They go on to be made perfect by the flesh." How is this ? Because, you see, the Spirit puts before every soul this walk of full consecration and whole-hearted devotedness to God, and instead of being obedient to the heavenly vision, the soul shrinks back and says, "That is too much — that is too close — that is too great a sacrifice"— and they decline, and instead of giving up a profession and going back into the world (there would be ten times more hope of them if they did this), they cling on to their profession and kindle a fire of their own, and walk in the sparks they have kindled. But He says He is against them, and "they shall lie down in sorrow." Oh ! there is a deal of this. People must have a God and a religion. They will have one, and when they shrink from the true one, and will not follow the Divine counsel, then they make one for themselves, and a great many of them go to sleep and never wake again. They go out of the world comfortably under the influence of narcotics, and they never wake. They die deceived; or, if they do awake, we know what sort of an awakening it is, and what sort of a deathbed theirs is. Our poor Salvation Army people — these "fishermen," — these young women — are sent for to pray with these people when they get awakened. And oh! what scenes are witnessed. Oh! see to it that you get awake and keep awake, and be willing to follow the Spirit's teaching in everything, at all costs and sacrifices.

I want you to note, first, how these people waited. "Tarry at Jerusalem till ye be endowed with POWER." Mark, that is not truth merely. They had got truth before. There is something besides truth needed. Paul says his Gospel and his preaching were not merely in word, but in *power*, and in the demonstration of the Spirit. What would be the first thing that would strike you that these disciples would be thinking of, as they wended their way back from Olivet, — having taken leave of their now glorified Master, — back again to the upper room at Jerusalem? Imagine what state of mind would be theirs. How would they wait for the promise?

Methinks the first feeling would be that of deep *self-abasement*. As they thought of the past; now that the full glory of His Divinity, and the Divinity of His mission had burst upon them, and, as they thought of their three years' sojourn with Him, and of all their darkness and blindness of heart, and all they had lost — all that they might have known — all He would have revealed to them, if they would have received it — as the thought of it all burst upon them just as, next day, when you find out who a person was, or some particular circumstance respecting a person that you did not fully understand at the time, and, when the person is gone, and it all breaks upon you, you say, " What a fool I was!" and so methinks these apostles would say.   Indeed, as he said, " Oh, fools, and slow of heart to believe ! "   They were cured — Peter certainly was — of self-sufficiency, of pride, and all of them would go back again in deep self-abasement.

Can you not think you see them as they assembled in the upper room ?   I should not be surprised at all if Peter, with his impulsive nature — and it is a glorious thing to have an impulsive nature when it is impulsive for good — to be zealously affected always in a good cause — threw himself on his face before his risen Master in deepest humiliation and broken-heartedness for his base ingratitude in having denied Him.   And how do you think Thomas and all of them would feel as they remembered the scene in the Garden, and how they all in the hour of His agony forsook Him and fled ?   How would they all feel ?   Oh! they would feel indeed unholy, untrue, cowards, and would go down, over and over again, on their faces, to wait in deep self-abasement.

And now, friends, this is the very first and indispensable condition of receiving the Holy Ghost.   You must first realize your past impurity, unholiness, disobedience, and ingratitude.   You must not be afraid to know the worst of yourselves.   You must look back at the time when your hand has been with Him on the table, and yet you have virtually betrayed Him.   You must look at your unfaithfulness and disobedience, at your shrinking from the cross, at your cleaving to the world, and if you want to be filled with the Spirit, you must be willing to know the worst of yourself, and tell the Lord the worst of yourself.   You must say, " Now,

Lord, am I low enough ?   Now, Lord, am I down far enough
in the dust for Thee to come and lift me up ?   I abhor myself.   I loathe myself in dust and ashes, and I want Thee to
come and fill me with Thy Spirit."   You will have to be
emptied of self.   When people are self-sufficient, God always leaves them alone to prove their self-sufficiency.   When
people think they can do for themselves, He lets them fall
down and see their weakness.   We must realize our utter
helplessness and weakness — we must be utterly lost in our
own sight.   Some of you, I think, have come to that, and
others are not quite low enough.   You must get down
lower, my brother.   God's way to exaltation is through the
Valley of Humiliation.   You must get lower — lower.   You
can never get too low in your own estimation in order to be
filled with the Spirit of God.

They waited, secondly, in earnest appreciation of its importance.   Ah! they had enough to make them do it.
How do you think they felt when they got into the upper
room ?   We are told that there were about 120 of them.
How do you think they felt as they thought of the past,
remembered the ignominious crucifixion of their Lord,
looked forward to the future, and contemplated the work to
which he had called them ?   And what was it ?   It was not
to go and set up an idol of Jesus Christ alongside of other
idols in the temples of heathen gods, but it was to go into
the city of Jerusalem, where they had just crucified Him
between two thieves, and proclaim Him as the long-expected
Messiah of the Jews.   It was to begin to set up this royal
spiritual kingdom in contradistinction to their temporal and
earthly kingdom, and then to go out from Jerusalem and
subjugate the world to His sway !   How would they feel ?
Poor Peter, and Thomas, and John, and Mary and the rest

of the women (thanks to the Holy Ghost, He has taken
care to put it in that they were there)— how would they
feel ?   They would feel, "We might as well stop and die
here, as go out as we are, until we do get the equipment of
power.   We want something more than we have got."   And
there they waited, and they said, "Lord, pour it out upon
us ; we are ready.   We are helpless, we are powerless — we
can do nothing.   Thou knowest what Thou hast called us to
do, and Thou hast promised this power to perform it.   Now,
here we are.   It is useless for us to begin until we get
power."   They appreciated its importance.   God never gave
this gift to any human soul who had not come to the point
that he would sell all he had to get it.   Oh ! it is the most
precious gift He has to give in earth or in Heaven — to be
filled with the Spirit, filled with Himself (as we said last
Sunday), taken possession of by God ; moved, inspired, ener-
gized, empowered by God, by the great indwelling Spirit
moving through all our faculties, and energizing our whole
being for Him.   This is the greatest and most glorious gift
He has.   He is not likely to give it to people who do not
highly appreciate it, and so highly that they are willing to
forego all other gifts for it — everything else, creature love,
creature comfort, ease, enjoyment, and aggrandizement for
this one thing.   Have you come to that ?   Are you telling
the Lord so ?   Are you sincere ?   If you are really sincere
in what some of you write me, then some of you have come
to it ; — but, oh, how people can deceive themselves !   My
heart has been greatly pained during this last week with one
or two instances of this kind that have come to my notice.
I have been half the week, I think, with Elijah under the
juniper tree.   I have cried, "Lord, who hath believed our
report?"   Who will thus take hold of God for this special

and full salvation? Alas! how few. One draws back for one reason and another for another. One feels how far they come with us. You can hear the tread of their feet, and you can hear how they falter and draw back. None but those who travail for souls can ever understand the agony of feeling that souls are drawing back when you have brought them on the road so far. I have thought many a time of the Saviour, when so many who had been hearing Him forsook Him and fled. It was after he had been trying to lead them higher, even to real spiritual union with Himself.

They were not willing to go all the way — to pay all the price — to suffer all the consequences — but, if you want this blessing, I know no other way. I had to come to this before I got it. The last idol of my soul had to be renounced, and it was hard work, as it always is, because we *love idols*. Idols would not be idols if they were not beloved. But we have to lay our real Isaac, our beloved and only Isaac, upon the altar. It is hard work, but it has to be done, because He is a jealous God. and will have no rivals. Do you so appreciate this blessing that you are willing to give up your Isaac? If so, you may have it this afternoon. He will fill you with His Spirit.

Third, and lastly, they waited *in obedient faith*. How do we know? Because t*hey did as He bid them* — that is the evidence. He said, " Go. tarry in the city of Jerusalem." Peter might have said, when he had seen his Lord off to Heaven, " Well, what am I going to do now? I have been a long time running after the Lord in Palestine, I must betake myself to the fishing. I can wait as well on the sea-beach as in Jerusalem. I wonder why the Lord told me to go to Jerusalem? I think·it was rather unreasonable. He

might have thought of my old father and mother at home.
I think I shall go back to my fishing-nets." No, no, they
had been cured of their unbelief by the last few days experience. They had learned better than to dictate to their
Master, and they knew He had a good purpose in sending
them to Jerusalem, and so they went there and did as He
bade them — straight back to that upper room they went.
Mary might have said, " I have been running about minister-
ing to the Saviour a long time, I'm afraid my friends will think
I am neglecting home duties and the claims of old friends.
I really must go home and see to matters a bit: I may as
well wait there for the Holy Ghost as at Jerusalem." No,
Mary had learned better. She went back to Jerusalem.
We have got their names. And they entered into the upper
room, and shut the door, and waited — obedient faith!
Some of your poets said —

> " Obedient faith that waits on Thee,
> Thou never wilt reprove."

No, it is the disobedient faith that is sent empty away.
Oh! people are crying out about their faith, but it is their
disobedient faith. If the Lord has told you to wait in any
particular place, or way, or company, or time, and you disobey Him, you will never get it, and you will have to come
to those conditions at last, even if it is on your dying bed!
Obedient faith! While there is a spark of insubordination,
or rebellion, or dictation, you will never get it. Truly
submissive and obedient souls only enter *this* kingdom.
Anywhere He tells you to go, anything He tells you to
sacrifice, or fly from, you will have to do. This is one of
His choice gifts that He has reserved for His choice servants, those who serve Him with *all their hearts.* Obedient
faith!

But you say, "How do you know it was faith? Oh, because we know they did as He bade them. Now faith is inseparable from expectation. Where there is real faith there is always expectation, and when I hear people praying, as I often do, *from their throats,* for the Holy Ghost, and see how they talk the minute they get up from their knees, and know how they live and whom they associate with, and how they spend their time, I say, " Yes, you may pray till your dying day, but you will never get it." If they expected anything, they would wait for it: common sense tells us that.

Those people waited. How long? What a hue and cry there is now about the Salvation Army people spending whole nights in prayer. People — Christians, grey-headed Christians, up and down the country — say to me, " I don't know how you get the time over. It must be such an immensely long time. Do you really mean to say that you spend all night in prayer?" I say, "Yes, with just an interval for putting the truth and showing the people how to apply it to their own consciences." Then they say, "It must seem an awfully long time." I suppose it does, to them, to spend one whole night in prayer; but here, we are told, they waited ten days, till the Day of Pentecost was fully come. I have no doubt they went as far into the night as they could keep their natural powers awake. They waited. They did not set the Lord a time. They were wiser. They did not say, "Now we will go and have a couple of days of it. That will be a long time. We will just shut out all else and wait on the Lord for a couple of days, and if He does not come by that time, it will be outrageous to wait beyond it. Whoever heard of a prayer-meeting two days and two nights long?" They did not set the Lord a time. They went and waited till it came.

You say, "No; I have not got it." No; because you did not wait until it came. You got hungry, or you fell asleep, or hugged your idol. You did not wait TILL IT CAME.

Suppose they had given up on the fifth day and said, "There must be some mistake. He knows we are here, all ready, and the world is perishing for our message. There must be some mistake. We had better begin." But no, they waited on, and on, and on, until it came. Can you imagine what sort of prayers went up from the upper room? Do you think they were the lazy, lackadaisical prayers that we hear every now and then for the Holy Spirit?

Oh! how would Peter agonize and wrestle! how would Thomas plead! how would Mary weep, beseech and entreat, and how were they all of one heart and of one accord. They wanted the one thing, and they were there to get it. They cared for nothing else but that. They cried for it as hungry children cry for bread. *They wanted it.* Did the Lord ever disappoint anybody who waited like that? Can anybody say so here? Did you ever hear of such a case? Never. HE CAME.

Oh! but there are some people, now-a-days, who set God times in everything. They think a good deal more about their dinners than about Him. They think a great deal more about intercourse with their friends and doing the polite to them, than they do about the precious waiting Holy Spirit of God. They think a great deal more about their businesses. "Oh!" they say, "it is business, and business must be attended to." But what about the Holy·Ghost and the Kingdom? Must not the Kingdom of God be attended to? Must not your soul be saved; and must you not become a temple of the indwelling Spirit of God? Put a MUST in there, if you please. Far more important is the soul than

the body.   Friends, are these things so, or am I only imag-
ining them?   Are these great truths, or are they fables?
These are the most commonsense, simple exhibitions and
illustrations of these truths that could possibly be given.
Was it not so?   Did they not thus wait, and did not the
Holy Ghost come? — and when He came, *He sat upon them
each.*   Bless his name!

People have a wonderful habit of losing sight of the little
words of the Bible — the people who make a great to-do
about the word in other ways, often say, "I never saw that
till you directed my attention to it."   Suppose I were to
say that this afternoon something happened to each person,
would you imagine I meant the men and not the women?
Of course you would say I meant everyone.   And it filled
them all — the women as well as the men, and they began
to speak with other tongues, as the Spirit gave them utterance.   *He came.*

And, my friends, He comes yet.   My bodily senses have
been quite cognizant of His coming sometimes.   We only
know that we feel something that so influences our bodies
that we cannot describe it.

In the North, when I was there, we had an all-night of
prayer, at which one thousand people, admitted by ticket,
waited all night on God.   The meeting began at ten, and
went on until six in the morning, and there were strong men,
men in middle life and old men, lying on their faces on the
floor.   There were doctors there, who examined them and
tried to account for it from physical causes, but they could
not.   *It was the power of God.*   The Holy Ghost *does* come,
and because, in coming thus into our souls, and thus filling
us, He sometimes prostrates our bodies, people rebel, as they
did on this occasion, and reject the manifestation, and say,

"Excitement! fanaticism!" What right have you to say that the Holy Spirit coming into a human soul can operate upon that soul to the full extent without, to some degree, prostrating the body? We know how people fall under great emotions of anger, grief, and joy. Why? Because the influence of the mind has so affected the body that the body cannot bear it, and when the Holy Spirit of God comes into a human soul and opens its eyes, and quickens its perceptions, and enlarges its capacity, and swells it with glory, is it an unlikely or improbable thing that the body should sometimes be prostrated under His power? What did Paul say?—"I bear in my body the marks of the Lord Jesus, and I have been into the third heaven and heard things that it was unlawful (or impossible) to utter." Do you think God intended such experiences and visions only for Paul and the apostles? Ah! there have been many since his day who have had such experiences, and many more of God's people *might* have them, if they would, but they are not willing to be wrapt in His arms; they are not willing to be pressed to His bosom; they are not willing to know Him in a Scriptural sense; they are not willing to be given up and consumed by His Spirit. Their heart and flesh do not cry out after the living God, as David's did. They are not panting after Him as the hart after the water-brooks. They are not longing to come and appear before God. If they were so longing that they could not live without it, then God would come to be revealed to them. Will you, then, wait in obedient faith?

Oh! I have the most awful realization that you will be eternally better or worse for these services, and so I want you to come up higher. I don't want you to go back, and get cold and indifferent to these things, because here is the hope of the world, if there is any hope for it, in people getting filled with the Spirit, people getting so woke up to God and His glory, and the interests of His kingdom, that they should be just as anxious for souls as other people are for sovereigns. Filled with the Spirit, having eyes to see spiritual sights which others do not see, ears to hear the crying of the famishing multitudes who are dying for lack of knowledge; hearts to feel so that they could go and weep over them. Hands to break the bread of life, and, if need be, a zeal that will lead them to die for them. This is what we want, and it only comes with the fulness of the Spirit.

Are you willing, my brother? Are you willing, my sister? If so, stop with us this afternoon. Never mind the dinner; never mind the tea. You have taken care of the outer man long enough, now look after the inner man. Never mind the children, mother, just now, the Lord will take care of them. Never mind anything, you who are athirst, but getting this blessed Holy Spirit of God, this full baptism of it on your souls. The Lord help you. Amen!

THE WORLD'S NEED.

"Son, go work to-day in my vineyard." — MATT. xxi. 28.
"And the Lord said unto the servant, Go out into the highways and hedges, and compel them to come in, that my house may be filled." — LUKE xiv. 23.

We might have enumerated other texts, teaching the same truth. There are plenty of them, but the general tenor and bearing of the Word of God, especially of the New Testament, is more significant than even direct and isolated texts. It seems to me that no one can disinterestedly and dispassionately study the New Testament without arriving at the conclusion that it is a fundamental principle, underlying the whole, that His light and grace is expansive: that is, God has, in no case, given His light, His truth, and His grace to any individual soul, without holding that soul responsible for communicating that light and grace to others. Real Christianity is, in its very nature and essence, aggressive. We get this principle fully exhibited and illustrated in the parables of Jesus Christ. If you will study them, you will find that He has not given us anything to be used merely for ourselves, but that we hold and possess every talent which He has committed to us for the good of others, and for the salvation of man. If I understand it, I say this is a fundamental principle of the New Testament.

How wonderfully this principle was exhibited in the lives

of the apostles and early Christians! How utterly careless they seemed to be of everything compared with this — this was the first thing with them everywhere! How Paul, at the very threshold, counted nothing else of any consequence, but willingly, cheerfully gave up every other consideration to live for this; and how he speaks of other apostles and helpers in the Gospel who had been nigh unto death, and laid down their necks for the work's sake; and we know how he travelled, worked, prayed, wept, and suffered, bled and died, for this one end. And so with the early Christians, who were scattered through the persecutions, how they went everywhere preaching the Word; how earnest and zealous they were, even after the apostolic age, we learn from ecclesiastical history — how they would push themselves in everywhere; how they made converts, and won real, self-denying followers even in kings' courts; how they would not be kept out, and could not be put down, and could not be hindered or silenced. " These Christians are everywhere," said one of their bitterest persecutors. Yes, they were instant in season and out of season; they won men and women on every hand, to the vexation and annoyance of those who hated them. Like their Master, they could not be hid; they could not be repressed, so aggressive, so constraining was the spirit which inspired and urged them on.

It becomes a greater puzzle every day to me, coming in contact with individual souls, how people read their Bibles! They do not seem to understand what they read. Well might a Philip or an angel come to them and say, "Understandest thou what thou readest?" Oh! friends, study your New Testament on this question, and you will be alarmed to find to what an awful extent you are your brother's keeper—to what an awful and alarming extent God holds you responsible for the salvation of those around you.

I want to glance, FIRST, at *our call to work for God ;* and, SECONDLY, at *two or three indispensable qualifications for successful labour.*

And, *first,* as I have just said, we are called by the Word not only in these direct passages, but by the underlying *principle* running through it all, and laying upon us the *obligation to save men.* In fact, the world is cast upon us ; we are the *only people who* CAN *save the unconverted.*

Oh! I wish I could get this thought thoroughly into your minds. It has been, perhaps, one of the most potent, with respect to any little service I have rendered in the vineyard,—the thought that Jesus Christ has nobody else to represent Him here but we Christians ; nobody else to work for Him. These poor people of the world, who are in darkness and ignorance, have nobody else to show them the way of mercy. If we do not go to them with loving earnestness and determination to rescue them from the grasp of the great enemy ; if we do not, by the power of the Holy Ghost, bind the strong man and take his goods, who is to do it? God has devolved it upon us. I say this is an alarming and awful consideration.

Secondly, we are called by the Spirit. The very first aspiration, as I said the other night, of a newly-born soul, is after some other soul. The very first utterance, after the first burst of praise to God for deliverance from the bondage of sin and death, is a prayer gasped to the throne for some other soul still in darkness. And is not this the legitimate fruit of the Spirit ? Is not this what we should expect ? I take any one here, who has been truly saved, to record if the first gushings of his soul, after his own deliverance, was not for somebody else — father, mother, child, brother, sister, friend?

Oh! yes, some of you could not go to sleep until you had written to a distant relative, and poured out your soul in anxious longings for his salvation;—you could not take your necessary food until you had spoken or written to somebody in whose soul you were deeply interested. The Spirit began at once to urge you to seek for souls; and so it is frequently the last cry of the Spirit in the believer's soul before it leaves the body. You have sat beside many a dying saint, and what has been the last prayer? Has it been anything about self, money, family, circumstances? Oh! those things are now all left behind, and the last expressed anxiety has been for some prodigal soul outside the kingdom of God. When the light of eternity comes streaming upon the soul, and its eyes get wide open to the value of souls, it neither hears nor sees anything else! It goes out of time into eternity, praying, as the Redeemer did, for the souls it is leaving behind.* This is the first and *last utterance* of the Spirit in the believer's soul on earth; and oh! if Christians were only true to the promptings of this blessed Spirit, it would be the prevailing impulse, the first desire and effort all the way through life. It is not God's fault that it is not so. In personal dealing with souls no point comes out more frequently than this: nothing which those who have really been converted and become backsliders in heart more frequently confess and bemoan than their unfaithfulness to the monitions of the Spirit with respect to other souls. In fact, backsliding begins here in thousands of instances. Satan gets people to yield to considerations of ease, propriety, being out of season, being injudicious, and

* Thus died David Stoner.

so on; and they lose opportunities of dealing with souls, and so the Spirit is grieved and grieved. Oh! what numbers of people have confessed this to me.

A gentleman, in advanced life, said: "When I was a young man, and in my first love, the zeal of the Lord's house so consumed me that I used to neglect my daily business, and could scarcely sleep at night; but alas! that was many years ago." "Was it not better with you *then* than *now?*" I asked; and the tears came welling up into his eyes. Oh, yes! the Lord says of him, "I remember thee, the kindness of thy youth, the love of thine espousals, when thou wentest after me in the wilderness, in a land *that was* not sown; Israel *was* holiness unto the Lord, *and* the first fruits of His increase." And, alas! there are many such to-day. They have it all to do over again; they have to repent and do their first works; they have to come back and get forgiven, and washed, and saved, if they are to go into the kingdom on high, all for want of systematically and resolutely obeying the urgings of the Holy Spirit towards their fellowmen.

Now, you have, some of you, been hearing, the last few Sundays, about grieving the Spirit, and about being filled with the Spirit; and some of you are puzzled as to how you ought to wait—whether you ought to go on with your lawful avocations and wait. I say: My friends, I could quite justify the position I took up last Sunday, but I will not stop, for I do not care about circumstantials; but mind, *this* is the great point—you must so wait, wherever it may be; so plead and wrestle, and believe, THAT YOU GET IT. Then I care not whether it be in Jerusalem, in the Upper Room, or anywhere else—*only, get it.* Don't let us lose the substance in quibbling about the way. Wait in that way congenial to your present circumstances; but, oh! wait for it until you get it, for this is the life of your souls, and the life of many souls, perchance, besides yours. You want this *spirit* — the spirit that yearns over the souls of your fellow-men; to weep over them as you look at them in their sin, and folly, and misery; the spirit that cannot be satisfied with your own enjoyments or with feeling that *you* are safe, or even that your children are safe; but that yearns over every living soul while there is one left unsaved, and can never rest satisfied until it is brought into the kingdom.

Such are the urgings of the Spirit; and if people would only be obedient to them, they would never lose these urgings. Why, what an anomaly it is! Does it look reasonable, or like God's dealings, that people should begin, like the old man felt when he was young, and, instead of waxing stronger, and having this holy zeal and desire *increased*, get weaker and weaker, and less and less? Does it look like God's way of doing things? Oh, no! This eclipse is through grieving and quenching the Spirit.

Now, my friend, you are called by the Spirit to this work. Obey the call — DO IT. Never mind if it chokes you — do it. Say, "I had better die in obedience than live in disobedience." Oh! these everlasting likes and dislikes. "I cannot speak to that person." "I cannot write that letter." "Oh! you don't know what would be the consequences." Never mind the consequences — do it. God will stand between you and the consequences; and, if He lets you suffer, never mind — then suffer; but obey the voice of the Spirit. There would have been thousands of souls saved if all those who have had these urgings had obeyed them. Pray, where do these urgings come from? Do they come from your own evil hearts? Then you are better than the

Apostle. Separated from the Spirit that dwells in you, and disunited from Christ, your living Head, you are selfish, *devilish*. Then where do these urgings come from? Do they come from the devil? Satan, then would indeed be divided against himself. Where do they come from? It is the Spirit of the living God that is urging you to come out and seek to save the lost. Will you obey these urgings? Will you give up your reasonings? Will you give up your likes and dislikes and OBEY? If you will, then He will come to you more and more, till, like David, you will feel the interests of his kingdom to be more to you than meat or drink, than silver or gold. Nay, you will become like him who said, "The zeal of Thine house hath eaten me up."

But, further, *we are called to this work by what He has done for us.* And what is that? Oh! you say, I cannot tell. No, no; we shall have to get *home* first, and then we shall never be able to tell. We shall never be able to cast up *that* sum, not even for the gratification of the angels. That will remain an unexplored quantity for ever, what He has done for us!! We shall have to find out what it would have been to have been lost! and what it is to be saved in all its fulness and eternity, before we can tell what He has done for us!!

What has He done for us? Oh! if we had a tithe of the love to sinners that He had for us, of His forbearing patience, of His persevering effort, when He followed us day and night, reasoned and reasoned with us, wooed and allured us, what could we not do?

I remember reading, somewhere, the story of a nobleman *
who was (I think) a backslider. He was stopping at some

* Count Zinzendorf.

country inn, and he went up into a room in which, over the mantelpiece, there was a very good picture of the crucifixion by a good old master, and under it was written, "I suffered this for thee — what hast thou done for me?" This question went home. It struck deep. He thought — Yes, what indeed? He went out into the stables to his horses, to try to get rid of the uncomfortable impression, but he could not forget it. A soft, pathetic voice seemed to follow him, — "I suffered this for thee — what hast thou done for me!" At last it broke him down, and he went to his knees. He said: "True, Lord, I have never done anything for Thee, but now I give myself and my all to Thee, to be used in Thy service."

And have you never heard that voice in your soul, as you have been kneeling at the Cross? Did you ever gaze upon that illustrious Sufferer, and hear His voice, as you looked back into the paltry past? What hast Thou done for me?

Now, there have been, at least, something like 350 people, who have come forward, so far, in these services, professing to give themselves afresh and fully to Jesus. I am sure, in the main, they have been sincere. They have come for the witness of the Spirit to their adoption, and for power for service. Now, friends, I want to know what this is to come to — what is to be the end of it?

> "What are you going to do, brother?
> What are you going to do?"

And sister, too. Is it going to die out in sentiment? Is it going to evaporate in sighs and wishings, and end in "I CANNOT"? God forbid! What are you GOING TO DO? What HAVE you been doing for Him the last week? Ask yourselves. You say — "Well, I have read my Bible more."

Very good, so far as it goes. What have you read it for?
"Well," you say, "to get to know the Lord's will and to get
instruction and comfort." Aye, exactly, but that is all for
yourself, you see. "I have prayed a great deal." Very
good. I wish everybody would pray. The apostles say all
men everywhere ought to pray. "I have been asking the
Lord for great things." Very good, praise the Lord; but
those are for yourself, mainly. If you have been led
out in agonizing supplication for souls, thank God for it, and
go on, and, as the Apostle says, "Labour thereunto, with all
perseverance, praying in the Holy Ghost;" but if it has been
merely to get all you can for yourself, what profit is that to
the Lord? But you say — "I am bringing up my family."
Exactly; so are the worldly people around you, but what
for? For God or for yourself? Oh! let us look at these
things, friends. I am afraid a great deal of religion is a
mere transition of the selfishness of the human heart from
the world to religion. I am afraid a great deal of the
religion of this day ends in getting all you can and doing as
little as you can — like some of your servants. You know
the sort, who will do no more than they are forced — just
get through, because they are hired. There is a great deal
of that kind of service in these days, both towards man and
towards God!

Now, friends, what have you been doing for Him — for
the promotion of *His* blessed, glorious, saving purposes in
the world? What have you been denying yourself for the
sake of His kingdom? What labor have you gone through
of mind, or brain, or heart? How many letters have you
written? How many people have you spoken to? How
many visits have you made? What self-denying labor have
you been doing for Him who has done (as you say) so much

for you? What have you been suffering for Him? Have you been trying, in some little measure, to fill up behind the measure of His sufferings "for His body's sake, the church?" Have you been carrying the sins and sorrows of a guilty world on your heart before God, and pleading with Him for His own Name's sake, to pour out His Spirit upon the ungodly multitudes outside, and to quicken half-asleep professors inside? Have you been subjecting yourself to reproach and contempt — not only from the world, but from half-hearted professors and Pharisees, bearing the Cross, enduring the shame of unkind reproaches in living and striving to save them? Oh, what have you been doing, brother and sister?

Come, now, friends, I want a practical result. He suffered that for you. He is up yonder, interceding for · you. Five bleeding wounds He always bears in the presence of His Father for you. If He were to forget you for a single moment, or cease His intercession, what would happen? What are you doing for Him? He has left you an example that you should follow in His steps. What were they? They were blood-tracked; they were humble steps. They were steps scorned by the world. He was ignored, and traduced, and rejected of men. He had not where to lay His head. He carried in His body and in His soul the sorrows and sufferings of all our race. He was a man of sorrows — not His own. He had no reason to be sorrowful. He was the Father's own beloved, and He knew it, but He was a man of sorrows, and acquainted with grief. The griefs of this poor, lost, half-damned world He bore, and they were sometimes so intolerable that they squeezed the blood through His veins. Have you been following in His footsteps, in any measure? He lived not for Himself.

He came not to be ministered unto, but to minister, and took upon Him the form of a servant. What are you doing? Oh! my friends, up, up, and be doing. Begin, if you have not begun — begin to-day. Ask Him to baptize you with His Spirit, and let you begin at once to follow Him in the regeneration of the Spirit. You are called by what He did for you!

Then, you are called by the wants of the world. I have said so much about this at other times that I will not say more now, only methinks it is a theme that is never exhausted, and never will be while there are any more sinners to save. Oh! the wants of the world! To me it is an overwhelming, a prodigious thought, that He shed His blood for every soul of man, and that as He hung there, He saw, under all the vileness, and sin, and ruin of the Fall — the human soul created originally in His own image, and capable of infinite and eternal development and progress. The soul to be rescued, washed, redeemed, saved, sanctified, and glorified — He saw this glorious jewel and He gave HIMSELF for it. Look at these souls. There is not one of them so mean, or vile, or base, but can be rescued by the power of His Spirit, and by His living, glorious Gospel brought to bear upon them. The Saviour, quoting from the Prophets, says, "Ye are gods (and adds) the Scriptures cannot be broken." He had no such little, mean, insignificant estimate of the worth of human souls as some people have now-a-days, who consign whole generations to hell without any bowels of mercy or compassion. Oh! the Lord fill us with the pity of Jesus Christ, who, when He saw the multitudes, wept over them.

Oh! friends, think of one such soul! What is your gold, or houses, or lands — what your respectability, what your reputation, what all the prizes of this world? We talk about it, but who realizes it — *who*, WHO? — the value of one precious, immortal soul saved, redeemed, sanctified. Oh, the wants of the world! They are dying, THEY ARE DYING!! When people come to me with their fastidious objections, I say — "My friend, all I know is — souls are dying, dying."

If your homes were being decimated by the cholera, you would not be very particular about the means you used to stay it, and if anybody came with objections to the roughness of your measures, you would say, "the people are dying, they are dying," and that would be the end of all argument. I say, they are dying, and they ARE to be saved. Satan is getting them: I want God to have them. Jesus Christ has bought them. He was the propitiation for the sins of the whole world. They belong to Him, and He shall have everyone I can reach, and everyone I can inspire others to reach also.

The world is dying. Do you believe it? You are called by the wants of the world. Begin nearest home if you like, by all means: I have little faith in those people's ministrations who go abroad after others, while their own are perishing at their firesides. Begin at home but do not end there. "Oh! yes," people say, "begin at home," but they end there; you never hear of them anywhere else, and it comes to very little what they do at home, after all. God has ordained that the two shall go together. Get them saved by all means, but somebody else saved as well. Set yourself to work for God. Go to Him to ask Him how to do it. Go to Him for the equipment of power, and then begin. Never mind how you tremble. I dare say your trembling will do more good than if you were ever so brave. Never mind the tears. I wish Christians would *weep* the Gospel into people; it would often go deeper than it does. Never mind if you do stammer. They will believe you when it comes from the heart. They will say, "He talked to me quite natural," as a man said, some time ago — wondering that he should be talked to about religion in a natural way; but mind, no mock feeling, for they will detect it in a minute. Go to the closet until you get filled with the Spirit, and then go and let it out upon them. Finney says, "I went and let my heart out on the people." Get your heart full of the living water and then open the gates and let it flow out. Look them in the face and take hold of them lovingly by the hand and say, "My friend, you are going to everlasting death. If nobody has ever told you till now — I have come to tell you. My friend, you have a precious soul. Is it saved?" They can understand that! not beginning in a roundabout way, but talking to them straight: — "Do you ever think about your precious soul? Is it saved? Are your sins pardoned? Are you ready to die?" Your rich neighbors and your servant girls and your stable-men alike, can understand that.

A lady said to my daughter, "I have begun talking to people about their souls in quite a different way to what I used. I begin asking them if they do not know they are sinners and if ready to die, and it produces quite a different effect." For one reason, she has her own heart full of the love and Spirit of God, and that burns her words in. Begin in that way and see what God will do through you, for, of course, I only recognise you as the instrumentality which He has chosen, and those who reflect upon the instrumentality, reflect upon His wisdom. You go and put your hand to the plough and He will give you strength to push it along.

The Lord help you to go home thinking about the wants of the world, and the next Sabbath we will consider the qualifications for labour.

SERMON X.

THE HOLY GHOST.

"**And,** behold, I send the promise of my Father upon you : but tarry ye in the city of Jerusalem, until ye be endued with power from on high." — LUKE xxiv. 49.

"But ye shall receive power, after that the Holy Ghost is come upon you.' ·· ACTS i. 8.

Friends who were present at former services will remember our line of thought, without my stopping to recapitulate. My chief reason for taking up this subject again, after having preached four sermons on it, is to meet the difficulties of some whom I believe to be anxious and honest enquirers. Taking those who have written and spoken to me as representatives of a class, it occurred to me that there might be many others in a similar state of mind, and it is a great joy to me if the Lord uses me to meet real difficulties, and to help those who are exercised by them into a higher state of grace, and a more thorough and complete devotion to the Lord. This is my end. God is my witness in every service.

Now, I do not want to make any reflections, and will not do so any further than I can help; but in dealing with such a subject we cannot avoid this, to a certain extent, as I have said before; if the truth reveals error, and if trying to get into a better track necessarily iń-some measure reflects on the old track — we cannot help it, and we must not eschew the former for the latter. It must be manifest, I think, to every

161

spiritual and thoughtful Christian that there is a great want somewhere in connection with the preaching of the Gospel, and the instrumentalities of the church at large. That there are many blessed exceptions I joyfully and gladly admit. No one hails them with greater gladness than I do. That there are blessed green spots here and there in the wilderness is quite true, and when these are gathered together and descanted on in articles, they look very nice, and we are apt to take the flattering unction to our souls that things are not so bad after all; but, when we come to travel the country over and find how few and far between these green spots are, and hear what a tide of lamentation and mourning reaches us all round the land as to the deadness, coldness, and dearth of Christian churches, we cannot help feeling that there is a GREAT WANT SOMEWHERE! This is not only my opinion but it is almost universally admitted, that, with the enormous expenditure of means, the great amount of human effort, the multiplication of instrumentalities during the past century, there has not been a corresponding result.

People say to me, on every hand, we have meetings without number, services, societies, conventions, conferences, but what comes of them all, comparatively? And I may just say here that numbers of ministers and clergymen, in private conversation, admit the same thing. In fact, none are more ready to admit this comparative lack of results than many dear spiritual ministers. They say, when talking with us behind the scenes — "Yes, it is a sad fact. I think I preach the truth. I pray about it. I am anxious for results, but alas! alas! the conversions are but few and far between." And then, not only are those conversions few, but in the mass of instances superficial — we should expect from such a putting of the truth as that we have been reading about, numerous and continual turnings to the Lord as in those days — we should expect men coming out openly from sin and from God-dishonoring courses, businesses, and professions — coming out from fashionable and worldly circles, abjuring the world, and literally and absolutely following Christ as in those days. That is what we have a right to expect, and yet how comparatively rare they are, so that when people do this, there is quite a commotion, and it is talked about all over the land. This, I say, is universally admitted, and it behooves us to ask before God, and with an earnest heart, yearning, desiring to improve this state of things — where is the lack, what is the want?

Note, secondly, this want is not the truth. Oh! what a great deal of talk we have about the truth, and not any too much. I would not yield to any man or woman in my love for this Bible. I love this Word and regard it as the stand-ard of all faith and practice, and our guide to live by; but it is not enough of itself. The great want is not the truth, for you see facts would contradict this theory. If it were the truth, then there would be no lack at this day, compared with other times, because we never had so much of the truth. There never was so much preaching of the truth, or such a wide dissemination of the Word of God, yet, comparatively, where are the results?— Further, not only as to quantity, but as to quality, am I discouraged. Not only are there com-paratively few conversions, but a great many of these are of a questionable kind. We should not only ask — are people converted, but what are they converted to? What SORT OF SAINTS ARE THEY? because, I contend, you had far better let a man alone in sin than give him a sham conversion, and make him believe he is a Christian when he is nothing of the kind. So you see we must look after the quality as well as

the quantity, and I fear, we have an awful amount of spuri-
ous production, and it behooves us — and I will for one, if I
were to be crucified for it to-morrow — be true to what the
Spirit of God has taught me on this point, I will never pan-
der to things as they are for fear of the persecution which
follows trying to put them right.   God forbid!

Then, I say, the lack is not truth.   There will be thousands
of sermons preached to-day — the truth, and nothing but the
truth.   Nobody will pretend to say they were not in perfect
keeping with the Word of God; and yet they will be perfect
failures, and nobody will know it better than they who preach
them!   These are facts.

I was talking, on this point, awhile ago, with a good man,
who said, "Ah! yes, I have not seen a conversion in my
church for these two years."   Now, what was the reason?
There was a reason, and I am afraid many might say the
same.   Yet there are the unconverted.   They come to be
operated upon.   Take a church where there is a congregation
of, say 800 or 1,000, suppose with a membership of 200 or
300.   What becomes of the 500 or 700 unbelievers, who come
and go, Sunday after Sunday, like a door on its hinges, neither better nor worse? — nay, God grant it might be so, but
they are worse.   They get enough light to light them down to
damnation, but they do not get enough power to lift them
into salvation.   What IS THE MATTER?   There must be
something wrong.   Will you account for it.   It ought to be
accounted for!   It ought not so to be.   God is not changed.
Surely He is as anxious for the salvation of men now as He
ever was.   Human hearts are not changed; they are neither
better nor worse; they are depraved, vile, devilish — just
the same.   The Gospel is just the same power it ever was,
rightly experienced, lived, and preached.   It is still the

power of God unto salvation. Then what is the matter? The truth is preached. The people hear it, and yet they remain as they were. Where is the lack?

Now, I say, and I most unhesitatingly assert, that the great want is POWER — this power of which we have been reading. And I want to remark, thirdly, that this power is as distinct, and definite, and a separate gift of God as was this Book, as was the Son, or any other gift which He has given us!

It is distinctly recognized, not only in our texts, but, as we read to you again and again, as a distinct and definite gift accompanying the efforts of those who live on the conditions on which God can give it to them. We cannot explain this gift, but it is the power of the Holy Spirit of God in the soul of the speaker accompanying His word, making it cut and pierce to the dividing asunder soul and spirit. "Ye shall receive power after that the Holy Ghost is come upon you."

"Ye shall be endued with," — not the truth, not faith (they had faith before that), but, "Ye shall be endued with power, and, as He says in another place, "which all your adversaries shall not be able to gainsay or resist." Though they may stone you, as they did Stephen, they shall be cut in their hearts, and made to feel the power of your testimony.

Now, I find people who go to work, which is all right, because the power comes to us in obedient faith; but they go trusting in their own efforts. They are without this endowment of power, and they see no result. The work is a comparative failure. Oh! what numbers of people have come to me who have been at work in different directions, in churches, as ministers, elders, deacons, leaders, Sabbath school teachers, tract distributors, and the like, confessing that they had been working for more or less lengthened periods, and had seen comparatively little result. They **say,** " Do you think this is right ? Do you think I ought to go on ? " Go on, assuredly, but not in the same track. Go on, most decidedly, but seek a fresh inspiration. There is something wrong, or you would have seen some fruit of your labour—not all the fruit. God does not give to any of us to see it all; but we do see enough to assure us that the Holy Ghost is accompanying our testimony. God's people have always done that when they have worked in conformity with the conditions on which the power can be given.

Now, this is how I account for the want of results—the want of the direct, pungent, enlightening, convicting, restoring, transforming power of the Holy Ghost; and I care not how gigantic the intellect of the agent, or how equipped from the school of human learning, I would rather have a little child, with the power of the Holy Ghost, hardly able to put two sentences of the Queen's English together, to come to help, bless, and benefit my soul, than I would have the most learned divine in the kingdom without it, for " it is not by might, nor by power, but by My Spirit." Oh ! that you would learn it. When you have learnt that, you will be made; when you experience it, you will lay hold on God. It is not by might — might of intellect, or learning, or eloquence, or position, or influence ; it is not by might, nor by power— man's power — of any sort, but by My Spirit. That is as true as it ever was. HERE IS THE SECRET OF THE CHURCH'S FAILURE! She is like Israel of old : " She hath multiplied her defenced cities and her palaces, but she hath forgotton the God of Israel, in whom her strength is." If you will read the history of the church from the beginning, you will find it is true what I say, that just to the degree that the church has increased in the material, she has decreased in the spiritual. I do not say it ought to be so ; I do not say that is a necessity. I only give you a significant fact that it has been so.

You say — "How do you account for it ? " I account for it because we poor, wretched, tiny, helpless creatures, cannot get anything good in the creature, but we begin to TRUST in it. But when God teaches us that we have nothing to trust in, when He makes us realize our own nothingness and utter helplessness, and gives us hold of Him with the grasp of despair, then we will begin to be of some use — and never till then. It is God that worketh in us and by us. The Apostle labours all the way through to show and convince everybody that it was God in him and not of himself at all. Though he could have preached with enticing words of man's wisdom, and, no doubt, had many a temptation to do it, as everybody has who has dipped into the flowery paths of human rhetoric and learning, but he eschewed this as he would the devil. He said, " no — this one thing I do "— putting aside absolutely all else, he went on straight to that work till they cut his head off.

I believe you do perceive, but, if you do not, take the Book and examine it yourself, — be at the trouble, — you will not get at the mind of the Lord without a great deal of trouble on these matters of power, spiritual union, and the like. Take the Bible with you on your knees before the Lord ; show Him the words, and say, " Now, Lord, show me the meaning of this." Wait, and there will come a voice from the excellent glory. There will come as light from the Shekinah, which will reveal it in your spiritual consciousness, and you will thus know that thing forever. You will be wiser than your teachers with respect to that particular point.

Further, you say, " Can we have this power equally with

the early disciples?" I say, reasoning by analogy, assuming that what God has done in the past He will continue to do in the future, is it not likely that He will give it to us, because we equally need it? — we poor things, in our day, as they did in theirs, we equally need it: first, because the character of the agents is the same. We are very much like them, and they were very much like us. This has often en-couraged me. If they had been men of gigantic intellects and extraordinary education, training, and position; if they had possessed all human equipment and qualifications, we might have looked back through the ages in despair, and said, "I can never be such as they were." Look what they were, naturally, apart from this gift of power. The Holy Ghost has taken care to give us their true characters. They were men of like passions, weaknesses, tendencies, liability to fall, with ourselves — just such poor, frail, weak, easily-tripped-up creatures, and, in many instances, unbelieving and diso-bedient, before Pentecost. Now, I say this is encouraging for us all.

You remember what Jesus said to Mary — "Go and tell my disciples AND PETER." Mary, perhaps, would have left Peter out after his shameful denial of the Lord; for fear of this, Jesus said, "Go and tell my disciples AND PETER."

Ah! there are some here saying, "But Peter was not so bad as I am." Well, we don't know anything about that, but, whether you are worse or not, the Holy Ghost is equal to the emergency. He can cure you. He can baptize you with His power. You may have denied Him, if not as Peter did, yet practically as bad. It makes no difference to God whether you have been a little bad or very bad; whether you have denied Him once or thrice, or whether you have denied Him with oaths and curses. If you will only come, and comply with the conditions, He will look on you, heal you, and baptize you with power. Did they not all forsake Him and flee, except a few poor faithful women? All the world forsook Him and fled in the hour of His extremity. "Ah!" you say, "well, I have done the same myself. I would not watch with Him one hour. I have betrayed Him before my friends and acquaintances in the world, where I have been brought into circumstances that have tested my fidelity. My courage has failed, and I have failed to witness for Him." Yes, I know and agree with you that it was base ingratitude. You were a traitor, indeed; but still, if you will come back, "Peter," and repent, and do your first works, He will receive you — baptize you with power. Oh! what they were before Pentecost, and what they were after! Poor Peter, who could not stand the questionings of a servant maid, who could not dare to have it said that he was one of the despised Nazarenes, what a valiant soldier he afterwards became for the Lord Jesus Christ, and how tradition says he was crucified for his Master at the last. Anyway, we know he was a faithful and valiant soldier to the end of his journey.

Now, this baptism will transform you as it did them; it will make you all prophets and prophetesses, according to your measure.

Will you come and let Him baptize you? Will you learn, once and forever, that it is not a question of human merit, strength, or deserving, at all, but simply a question of submission, obedience, faith.

Then we need it because not only are the agents the same, but our work is essentially the same.

It may differ in its outward manifestations because we live in an age of greater toleration, but it is just the same in es-

sence, and I do not know, as to the manifestation, when **you**
come to do it in apostolic fashion, with apostolic spirit,
whether you do not get very much the same apostolic treatment. They gnash upon you with their teeth, and do **as**
much as the law will let them, and sometimes a little more,
in the way of stoning and persecuting you.

The great thing to be done by this power of God is to subdue the naturally evil, wicked, and rebellious heart of man.
Now God alone is able to do that. That is a superhuman
work. You may enlighten a man's intellect, civilize his
manners, reform his habits, make him a respectable, honest,
industrious member· of society, without the power of God,
but you cannot transform HIS SOUL. That is too much for
any human reformer. That is the prerogative of the Holy
Ghost, and I have not a shadow of a doubt that the eternal
day will reveal every other kind of work to be wood, hay,
stubble. All the sham conversions, all the people whose lives
and opinions have been changed by anything short of this
power, will be wood, hay, stubble. It is the prerogative of the
Spirit of God. Therefore, God never pretends to do it by
any other means ; and all through the Bible this power is as-
cribed to the Spirit of God. Therefore, we want this Spirit
to do this work. What! you set yourself to enlighten a darkened human soul, to convince a hardened, rebellious sinner, **to**
convert a rebel in arms against God, with an inveterate hatred
in the very core of his soul against God and all about God!
You set yourself to bring down *that* — to transform that evil,
wicked heart, to subdue that soul to submission and obedience!—you try it, try it without the Spirit of God! Oh!
no, you want that Spirit. You want the same measure of
that Spirit, just the same, which Paul had.

And what is our work? To go and subjugate **the world**

to Jesus; everybody we can reach, everybody we can influ ence, and bring them to the feet of Jesus, and make them re. alize that He is their lawful King and lawgiver; that the Devil is a usurper, and that they are to come and serve Christ all the days of their lives. Dare any of us think of it without this equipment of power? Talk about "Can we have it?" — we are of no use without it. What can we do without it? This is the reason of the effeteness of so much professed Christianity; there is no Holy Ghost in it. It is all rotten. It is like a very pretty corpse — you cannot say there is this wanting or the other wanting, it is a perfect form, but *dead*. It is like a good galvanic battery. It is all right — perfect in all its parts — but when you touch it there is no effect — there is no fire or shock. What is the matter? It only wants the fire — the power.

Oh! friends, we want the power that we may be able to go and stretch ourselves upon the dead in trespasses and sins, and breathe into him the breath of spiritual life. We want to be able to go and touch his eyes that he may see, and speak to the dead and deaf with the voice of God and make them hear. This is what we want — POWER.

If we equally need it, *is it likely that God will withhold it?* The Book, rightly read and understood, is full of prom- ise and exhortation to get it, Is it likely that if we are as frail as they were, if the work is the same, is it likely that the God of all grace, and our Father as much as theirs, and as much in sympathy with the souls of men, will withhold it from us? No, no. But our Saviour distinctly told us that He bought it for us — that it was more expedient that His people should have it than that He should remain with them. It is promised to all believers to the end of time. The conditions you know — simply putting away everything that hinders, casting aside every doubtful thing, trampling it in the dust; then a full, whole-hearted surrender to Him, embracing the Cross, embracing His' will at all costs and sacrifices, and then a determined march to the upper room at Jerusalem and a determined abiding there until you get it — these are the conditions. Anybody can have it on these terms.

Then, in conclusion, let me remind you — and it makes my own soul almost reel when I think of it — that God holds us responsible. He holds you responsible for all the good you might do if you had it. Do not deceive yourself. He will have the *five* talents with their increase. He will not have an excuse for *one*, and you will not dare to go up to the throne and say, "Thou wast a hard master, reaping where Thou dost not sow, and gathering where Thou hadst not strewn. Thou biddest me to save souls when Thou knewest I had not the power." What will He say to you? "Wicked and slothful servant, out of thine own mouth will I judge thee. You knew where you could have got the power. You knew the conditions. You might have had it. Where are the souls you might have saved. Where are the children that I would have given you? Where is the fruit?" Oh! friends, these are solemn and awful realities. Oh, what you might do! Who can tell? Who would ever have thought, twenty years ago, when I first raised my voice, a feeble, trembling woman, one of the most timid and bashful the Lord ever saved, the hundreds of precious souls that would be given me! I only refer to myself because I know my own case better than that of another; but, let me ask you — supposing I had held back and been disobedient to the Heavenly vision, what would God have said to me for the loss of all this fruit? Thank God, much of it is al-

ready gathered into Heaven, people who have sent me word
from their dying beds, that they blessed God they had ever
heard my voice, saying that they should wait for me on the
other side, prepared to lead me to the throne — what would
have become of the fruit? *I* should not have had it anyway. They would never have become *my* crown of rejoicing in the day of the Lord. Oh, who can tell what God
can do by any man or woman, however timid, however
faint, if only fully given up to Him. My brother, my sister, He holds you responsible. He holds you responsible,
my sister — you, who wrote me about your difficulties and
temptations in testifying of Jesus — He holds you responsible. What are you going to do? Ask yourself. It is
coming. You believe it! You say you do. Unless you
are a confirmed hypocrite, you do — that you are going to
stand before the throne of His glory. You believe that
you are going to stand before Him by-and-bye, when you
shall receive according to the things you have done in your
body. What shall you say? The world is dying — souls
are being damned at an awful rate every day. Men are
running to destruction. Torrents of iniquity are rolling
down our streets and through our world. God is almost
tired of the cry of our sins and iniquities going up into His
ears. What are you going to do, brother? What are you
going to do? Will you set to work? Will you get this
power? Will you put away everything that hinders?
Will you have it at all costs?

We had a letter very recently, about a gentleman who had
been reconverted in the services of the Salvation Army, telling us that he has relinquished an income of £800 a year,
in order to keep a conscience void of offence — this is
the result of the power of the Holy Ghost. I heard

of another gentleman who was invited to a party. After dinner, the card-table was got out, as usual, and when the cards were all spread and everybody was ready to begin, this gentleman jumped up, and pushed it away, and said, "I have done with this for ever." The lady who told me said, "He was down on his knees before we had time to turn round, and was praying for us and for all the house. Oh!" she added, "you should have seen them." Yes, of course, every man felt like the people round the Saviour. Every man's own conscience condemned him. "They went off home, without any more card-playing, or dancing, or wine-drinking that night." Come out from amongst the ungodly. Testify against them. Reprove them. Entreat them with tears; but be determined to deliver your soul of their blood. God will give you the power, and He holds you responsible for doing this. You have received the light. WILL YOU DO IT? If you will, we shall meet again, and rejoice with joy unspeakable. If you do, we shall praise God for ever that He brought us inside the walls of this building long after it has smouldered into dust. There shall be children and grandchildren, and great grandchildren from you spiritually, if you will only be faithful.